FGD SYSTEM

AN INITIATIVE TOWARDS CLEANER ENVIRONMENT

SHAILENDRA BHARDWAJ

ISBN 979-888503661-0

Dedicated to

My Father Late Sh. Surendra Mohan Sharma & My Mother Mrs Pushpa Sharma

Contents

Preface

The book demystifies the practical aspects of FGD System and sincere efforts were made to minimize inclusion of bookish knowledge. This compilation has facilitated capturing of knowledge and experience of already trained and experienced professionals for the benefit of the budding power engineers. This book will serve as ready reckoner for not only new entrant but also to experienced engineers of Power Plant.

In first two chapters, the book covers overview & Indian Scenario of FGD System. It covers Environment notifications, timelines, already installed capacity & future plans. Third & fourth chapters throw light on types of FGD Systems and detailed description of system, sub systems, chemical reactions etc. of wet FGD System. Chapter five focuses on cost of FGD Sytem, Limestone requirement and Gypsum Generation.

Chapter six explains civil works including Geotech Investigation, Piling, Wellpoint Dewatering, Chimney Erection through slipform, Flue Can erection, Borosilicate lining etc. Chapter seven decodes Absorber sizing, Absorber material and erection philosophy. Chapter eight breaks down the control philosophy of the FGD System including three major & seven minor control systems.

Chapter nine enlightens the readers with Learnings. These Learnings can help everyone working in the field of FGD erection & planning. Chapter ten covers the typical calculations of Limestone requirement and Gypsum production.

The facts written in this book were collected from different sources during more than 18 years of my job in power sector. To find the original sources of these facts and to write them in a table is nearly impossible. As power sector is dynamic, all readers are kindly requested to also read the Operation & Maintenance (O&M) Manual, Technical Specifications & Erection Manual of Original Equipment Manufacturer (OEM) while referring this book. As this is my second technical book, so despite of all the efforts if there is any mistake in the book, I am truly sorry.

Acknowledgements

To say the book is "by Shailendra Bhardwaj" overstates the case. Without the significant contributions made by other people, this book would certainly not exist.

At the top of the list is Sh. A. K. Sinha, Former Executive Director (Engg), NTPC Ltd. I was truly blessed to have such an extraordinary man to guide me. I hope this effort meets his expectation. Any shortcomings to reach that standard rest entirely upon me.

When I started off with this book, I was familiar with my intent and content but I didn't have an iota of ease in plunging into this unfamiliar terrain of book writing. I would like to thank Sh. Yougal Dhiman & Sh. Ganesh Nim for their belief in me and their unprecedented contribution in making of this book. I would like to thank Sh. Hari Prasad Joshi, CGM(Mouda) and Sh. B V Bhaskar, GM(TS) for the constant motivation & support.

In addition, I would like to thank Sh. Skandh & Sh. Ajit Chintankar, who were instrumental in learning concepts for writing this book.

I would also like to thank my wife Anjali and my sons Nabhya & Pranshul for their whole hearted support & love, without which writing this book was impossible.

I would like to thank all the readers of my two books, "**Power Plant – Soch se Safalta tak**" & "**Mill Maintenance: Converting Challenges into Opportunities**" for their encouragement, which motivated me to write this book.

About The Author

With more than Eighteen years of experience in Power Sector, Sh. Bhardwaj is a Mechanical Engineer (BE - Hons.) by profession. He is a researcher by interest, innovator by creative insight and is currently Senior Manager in NTPC Ltd, A Maharatna Company of Government of India. He Worked in Reliance Industries Ltd, Jamnagar, Gujarat (Gas Power Plant) & DCM Shriram Industries Ltd, Kota, Rajasthan (Thermal Power Plant) before joining NTPC. In last over 15 years in NTPC, he worked at Farakka Super Thermal Power Station, West Bengal, Feroze Gandhi Super Thermal Power Station, Unchahar, UP, Engineering Division at Corporate Centre, Noida and currently he is working at Mouda Super Thermal Power Project, Nagpur.

Sh. Bhardwaj, an upholder of professionalism, is MBA from ICFAI University, PGDBA from Symbiosis, Pune, Diploma in Training & Development from ISTD, Delhi, Certified Boiler Operation Engineer from Govt. of Rajasthan, Certified Welding Inspector from WRI, BHEL, Trichy, Accredited Energy Auditor from Bureau of Energy Efficiency and IRCA UK Certified QMS Lead Auditor. He has completed Executive Diploma in Project Management (EDPM) from International Institute of Projects & Program Management (I2P2M).

His experience is in the area of concept to commissioning of new thermal and solar projects. He also has extensive experience in Design, Erection & Commissioning and Maintenance of Mechanical Systems of Power Plant. He has experience of Planning & Systems of thermal power plants and worked with Industry Leaders. He is a Visiting Faculty in Employee Development Centres

& Power Management Institute for Technical & Managerial Trainings.

Sh. Shailendra is a voracious reader and enjoys Literature, Sports, Music, Dancing, Trekking, Marathon running and Motorcycle Tours. His Book, "**Power Plant: Soch se Safalta Tak**" got awarded from NTPC Ltd. His Managerial & Technical articles found places in Horizon, GETS, Mouda Darpan & Vidhyut Swar. He has won number of prizes & gold medals while participating in presentation competitions of national repute. He also won many tournaments in Billiards, Chess, Football and Cricket. He got number of appreciation letters not only from NTPC Ltd but also from BHEL, Dale Carnegie, Royal Enfield etc.

CHAPTER ONE

OVERVIEW

The combustion of fossil fuels, such as Coal and Heavy Fuel Oil (HFO), liberate three of the major air pollutants, such as sulfur dioxide (SO_2), nitrogen oxides (NO_X), and particulates. Carbon monoxide, sulfur dioxide, nitrogen oxides, volatile organic compounds and particulates are commonly referred as "criteria pollutants" because of their contribution to the formation of urban smog. Sulphur dioxide is a major pollutant and have a significant impact on human health. High concentrations of sulphur dioxide in atmosphere can influence the flora and fauna. Electrostatic precipitators or cyclones can satisfactorily remove Particulates, whereas the nitrogen oxides emissions can be reduced using low NOX burners & use of Selective catalytic reduction (SCR)/ Selective non-catalytic reduction (SNCR). In coal based thermal power plants, during the combustion process, about 95% of the sulfur is converted to sulfur dioxide (SO_2), which reacts with the particles of water in the atmosphere, forming acid rain under normal conditions of temperature and pressure. Sulfur dioxide emissions can be reduced by three methods in the process i.e. the removal of sulfur from the fuel before combustion, by the removal of sulfur dioxide during the combustion process, or by the removal of sulfur dioxide from the flue gases after combustion. The pre-combustion controls comprise selection of low sulfur fuels and fuel desulfurization. For conventional coal-fired plants, the combustion controls mainly involve in-furnace injection of sorbents. The most popular post-combustion controls are the Flue Gas Desulfurization (FGD) System.

The FGD Systems Market is projected to grow from USD 17.7 billion in 2020 to USD 23.1 billion by 2025, at a CAGR of 5.5% from 2020 to 2025. Market growth is driven by the enforcement of laws and regulations that mandate SOx emitting industries to install air quality control equipment. As coal-fired power plants are the chief contributor of flue gases, most countries have strict emission standards for power generation units, mandating them to install FGD systems with high removal efficiency. The flue gas desulphurization can be done both by wet or dry process. Based on type, the wet FGD systems segment is estimated to lead the market as these are the most used in industrial plants owing to their high removal efficiency (>95%). The most widespread process, wet desulphurization of limestone or lime, accounting for about 85% of all desulphurization processes. In the FGD market throughout the world, limestone wet scrubbers take the lead, the by-product of which is a marketable gypsum.

Shortly after the turn of the century, the sulfur in coal combustion gases was accepted as a source of sulfur in the production of sulfuric acid. Technological advances were made in SO_2extraction methods. However, the greatest contribution to modern applications was the recovery of sulfur in a commercially usable form. Studies related to the removal of sulfur dioxide (SO_2) from flue gases began in the 1860s when experiments were performed on

SO_2absorption in water. The first major FGD unit at a utility was installed in 1931 at Battersea Power Station, owned by London Power Company.

CHAPTER TWO

INDIAN SCENARIO

India satisfies most of power requirement through thermal power. Thermal power generation constitutes about 60% of the total installed capacity followed by renewable energy, which is 26.4% as on 31stOct'21. Installed capacity of Coal Based power plants is 202.41 GW as on 31.10.21. Indian coal is high in ash but is low in sulphur. Indian coal contains sulphur in the range of 0.25% to 0.5%. This range of sulphur content coal produces SO_2in the range of 1,500-2,000 microgram per cubic metre of flue gas (mg/Nm^3). However, coal is also imported from Indonesia, Australia and South Africa for fuelling thermal power plants. This imported coal is high in sulphur content while being low in ash. North-eastern Coal is also high in sulfur.

The Indian government has focused on reduction of emissions from coal based thermal power plants in accordance with the Intended Nationally Determined Contributions (INDCs) submitted to the United Nations Framework Convention on Climate Change (UNFCCC) that has committed to curb emission intensity of its economy by 30-35 per cent from the 2005 level by 2030.

Accordingly, the Ministry of Environment, Forest and Climate Change (MoEF & CC), has issued notification no: S.O.3305(E) titled 'Environmental (Protection) Amendment rules, 2015' dated 7.12.2015 with the objective of reducing emissions of suspended particulate matter (SPM), SOx, NOx and mercury at thermal power plants (TPPs). Prior to MoEFCC order, there were no norms for emission control of SO_2.

According to the amendment, the Thermal Power Plants has to comply the following norms specifically on Sulphur Dioxide (SO_2) emission:

- Units with capacity less than 500 MW and installed till 31st December 2016 – 600 mg/Nm^3
- Units with capacity equal to 500 MW and above and installed till 31st December 2016 – 200 mg/Nm^3
- Units which are being installed after 1st January 2017 – 100 mg/Nm^3

TPPs (units) shall meet the limits within two years from date of publication of this notification. Further, to the above MOEF & CC notification, MOEF &CC has subsequently issued an amendment dated 28th June 2018 for stack height post FGD:

Stack Height/Limit in Meters –

a. Power Generation capacity: 100 MW and above

$$H = 6.902\ (QX0.277)^{0.555}$$

Or

100 m Whichever is more

b. Less than 100 MW

$$H = 6.902 (QX0.277)^{0.555}$$

Or

30 m Whichever is more

Q = Emission rate of SO_2in kg/hr

H = Physical stack height in meter

As per the timelines for implementation of new emission norms for Thermal Power Plants (notified on 07.12.2015) prepared by Central Electricity Authority (CEA) as per direction issued on 11.12.2017 and 06.04.2018 u/s 5 of EP Act, 1986, the existing TPPs are required to comply with the new emission standards by the year 2022. However, many organisations formally requested CEA to give additional time to achieve the target. With the MoEF&CC order, it has become compulsory to install Flue Gas Desulphurisation (FGD) system in the existing and upcoming thermal power plants to curb SOx emissions.

The Ministry of Environment, Forest and Climate Change (MoEF & CC), has again issued notification no: G.S.R. 243(E) titled ‘Environmental (Protection) Amendment rules, 2021’ dated 31.03.2021. Through this notification a task force shall be constituted to categorise thermal power plants in three categories. The notification also gave details of penalty to be levied as environment compensation in case of non-adherence of timeline. The categories are explained as below:

S. No.	Category	Location/Area	Timeline for compliance	
			Non-Retiring Units	Retiring Units
1	Category A	Within 10 km radius of NCR or cities having million plus population	Up to 31.12.2022	Up to 31.12.2022
2	Category B	Within 10 km radius of critically polluted areas or non-attainment cities	Up to 31.12.2023	Up to 31.12.2025
3	Category C	Other than those included in A or B	Up to 31.12.2024	Up to 31.12.2025

Table-1: thermal power plants categories

Later CPCB issued minutes of the 3rd meeting of the Task Force on 27.08.2021, in which task force also published the list of 545 units, for which categorisation is agreed by task force.

First Flue Gas De-Sulphurisation stream (FGD) was commissioned in 1986 at Trombay and another stream was added in 1994 on unit 5. Two third (66%) of total flue gases are treated for SO_2removal here. The scrubber efficiency (SO_2removal efficiency) is observed at 90% against the manufacturer's guarantee of 85% removal. Being a coastal station, Trombay FGD is designed to work on sea water process, using untreated seawater to scrub the flue gas, exploiting the water's natural alkalinity to neutralize the SO_2. The chemistry of the process involves bicarbonate from the sea water reacting with the $SO_2$and oxygen (from the aeration process) to form Sulphate.

The country's largest power producer NTPC is installing sulphur dioxide-reducing technology flue-gas desulphurisation (FGD) at all its plants across the country. State-owned NTPC commissioned the Wet FGD technology at the 500-megawatt (MW) unit number 13 (stage V) unit at its 4,760 MW Vindhyachal power plant in 2017. NTPC also commissioned FGD System (DSI), in Stage – I units (4 x 210 MW) of Dadri Power Station. NTPC Limited will install FGD in 155 units of 64854 MW capacity, out of which FGD in 6 units of 1890 MW are under tendering, FGD commissioned in 5 units and awarded in rest of the units.

Jhajjar Power Limited (JPL), a subsidiary of CLP India, is the first private sector plant in the National Capital Region to have installed Flue Gas Desulphurisation (FGD) technology in Nov' 2020.

As on 31.10.21, total commissioned FGD capacity in India is 2660 MW. As per Annual Report 2019-20 of CEA, the total capacity for monitoring the implementation of FGD as on 31-03-2020 is 165942 MW & no. of units are 437 after including the units commissioned after 31-08-2017.

CHAPTER THREE

TYPES OF FGD SYSTEM

The flue gas desulfurization (FGD) plant removes sulfur dioxides (SO_2) from flue gas produced by boilers, furnaces, and other sources. SO_2emission results in:

- Decrease visibility by absorbing or diffracting sun light in the atmosphere along with floated particles.
- Incidence of chronic diseases at eyes, nose, neck or bronchus by exposure for long time.
- Decrease production and growth of plants by interrupting photosynthesis due to the black spot or chlorosis.
- Destruction of ecosystem by acidifying land or river due to acid rain or acid snow and corroding architectures.

There are various technologies, which are in use for De-Sox treatment of flue gases from thermal power plant. FGD processes are majorly divided in two categories i.e. Wet FGD and Dry/ Semi Dry FGD. FGD can be divided into the following five methods:

1. Spray dry scrubbers
2. Sorbent injection process
3. Dry scrubbers
4. Sea water scrubbing
5. Wet scrubbers

Next chapter will cover Wet scrubbers or Wet FGD in detail as this is the most widely used technology in the FGD market with over 80% of the installations by power plant capacity. Wet scrubbers can achieve removal efficiencies up to 99% and are preferred in Large & Medium Scale applications. Highlights of other methods are explained below:

1. **Spray dry scrubbers:**

This is the second most used method of FGD in the industry. The sorbent usually used is lime or calcium oxide (CaO). The lime slurry is atomised by spraying it into a reactor vessel in a cloud of fine droplets. The residence time (typically 10 seconds) in the reactor is sufficient to allow for the sulfur dioxide (SO_2) and other acid gases such as $SO_3$and HCl to react with the hydrated lime to form a dry mixture of calcium sulphate ($CaSO_4$) and calcium sulphite ($CaSO_3$).

Wastewater treatment is not required in spray dry scrubbers because the water is completely evaporated in the spray dry absorber by the heat of the flue gas. This process requires the use of an efficient particulate control device such as an ESP or fabric filter. The absorber construction material is usually carbon steel making the process less expensive in capital costs compared with wet scrubbers. However, the necessary use of lime in the process increases the operational costs. Spray dry scrubbers are limited in size compared to wet scrubbers. Normally the largest plant size for the spray dry scrubbers is around 200MW.

Spray dry scrubbers achieve removal efficiencies up to 97%. In this system, the capital cost is low, APC is low and system availability is high.

2. **Sorbent injection processes:**

In this system, Limestone ($CaCO_3$) or hydrated lime ($Ca(OH)_2$) is injected to react with sulfur dioxide (SO_2). This is injected either in the upper part of combustion chamber or in the economiser section of the boiler or in the flue gas duct downstream after the air preheater.

The sulfur being captured from the flue gas ends up as either calcium sulphate ($CaSO_4$) or calcium sulphite (CaSO3). This is later captured in a fabric filter or ESP together with unused sorbent and fly ash. The capital cost of the system is low and less time is required for installation & commissioning.

The FGD technologies based on dry sorbent injection is particularly preferable for small unit size i.e. 60 MW-250 MW range since the reagent cost in this technology is relatively higher then Wet-lime stone and ammonia based FGD, hence units running on low PLF and with less balance operating life (07-09 years) is more preferable for DSI.

3. **Dry scrubbers:**

Dry sorbent injection for reducing the SO_2emission is commonly used in Circulating Fluidised Bed or Moving Bed combustion boilers. Hydrated lime ($Ca(OH)_2$), limestone

($CaCO_3$) or dolomite ($CaCO_3 \cdot MgCO_3$) are commonly used for this purpose. The sorbent is injected into the bed zone where the combustion reactions take place. The sulphur of the fuel is captured as calcium sulphate ($CaSO_4$), which is retained in the ash. A typical SO_2removal efficiency is in the range of up to 99%. The capital cost of the system is low and SO_2removal efficiency is high. There are two main disadvantages of this system:

- The large quantities of sorbent required which is approximately twice that of a wet scrubber system to achieve the same SO_2 removal.
- The large quantities of strongly alkaline waste produced, which is generally disposed of in a landfill.

4. **Sea water scrubbing:**

In this system, acid gases are absorbed by the natural alkalinity of seawater. Sea water contains sodium (Na), magnesium bicarbonate ($Mg(HCO_3)_2$), and small quantities of calcium bicarbonate ($Ca(HCO_3)_2$). The flue gas flows through an absorption tower with a counter current flow of seawater. During this process, $SO_2$is absorbed by the seawater, before passing to a water treatment plant where further seawater is added to increase the pH. Air is supplied to oxidise the absorbed $SO_2$to sulphate (SO_4^{2-}) and to saturate the seawater with oxygen. The seawater is then discharged to the sea.

This system is simple, reliable and removes up to 99% of SO_2. It comes with low capital and operational costs and have no solid by-products. However, heavy metals and chlorides, if not removed before the SO_2capture, are present in the water released to the sea. This system is always preferable for FGD plants situated near sea.

5. **Wet Scrubbers:**

Wet scrubbers are the most widely used FGD technology for SO_2control throughout the world. Calcium-sodium based sorbents are used in a slurry mixture, which is injected into a specially designed vessel to react with the SO_2in the flue gas. Wet scrubbers can achieve removal efficiencies as high as 99%. The preferred sorbent in operating wet scrubbers is limestone ($CaCO_3$), followed by lime (CaO). In a lime/ limestone/ gypsum wet scrubber, the process is designed to produce a high-quality product (gypsum) suitable for use as raw material in various industries.

Wet FGD System:

The Wet FGD process involves passing the flue gas through a tower (also called Absorber) where an alkaline sorbent slurry is sprayed over the flue Gas (or the flue gas is bubbled through a sorbent slurry). The $SO_2$and other soluble gases are dissolved into the Slurry and clean gas exits the tower. Wet scrubbers use calcium, sodium, and ammonium-based sorbents in a slurry mixture with water, which is injected into to the scrubber to react with the sulfur dioxide (SO_2) in the flue gas. The preferred sorbent in operating wet scrubbers is limestone followed by lime. The wet process normally yields a useful by-product like gypsum, ammonium bisulphate etc. depending on the sorbent used. Gypsum slurry is bled off to a dewatering system where the moisture in gypsum is removed and gypsum is transported for storage/ sale.

The FGD technologies based on limestone slurry as reagent are most versatile and prominent for any unit size.

However, for optimum selection of technology plant specific factors like Unit size, balance unit life, space availability, saleability of by-product etc. needs to be considered. Limestone technology have large footprint, relatively higher CAPEX and Reagent purity issues while comparing with Ammonia based and dry type FGD technologies.

Dry Sorbent Injection (DSI) System:

The Dry Sorbent Injection (DSI) System is designed to pneumatically convey dry free flowing sorbent (Sodium Bicarbonate (SBC)) from SBC Silo, into a Loss-in-Weight (LIW) feed system, into a RVF and RAL, through the Viper Mill, to the splitters, and through the injection lances which are located in the Air Pre-Heater (APH) inlet duct.

In the DSI system, the Rotary Vane Feeder (RVF) is a device, which provides a means of transporting a material vertically in a vertical gravity fed line as well as volumetrically meter that material. A RVF is located below the Weigh Hopper and is used to adjust the material feed rate in the injection line using a variable frequency drive. The Rotary Air Lock (RAL) equipped below the RVF allows sorbent to be fed from the low pressure in the Weigh Hopper to the high pressure in the injection line. The RAL is equipped with a purge kit and a vent line that ties into the Weigh Hopper. The Viper Mill refines the sorbent to a smaller particle size. This increases surface area allowing for more efficient use of the sorbent. Splitters are Conveyor line equipment, responsible for splitting the material/ conveying air mixture and distributing it evenly among the injection lances. Injection lances are devices that are inserted into the APH inlet duct work that distribute the sorbent inside of the duct work. The injection lances are designed for easy removal from the ports for inspection and maintenance access.

There is one SBC Silo, 2 x 100% Viper Mills, each mill has a dedicated bypass, and 1 x 100% Conveying Line in the DSI system. This system uses 2 x 100% injection blowers along with dedicated condensing units and heat exchangers for the purpose of conveying the SBC from SBC silo to ductwork. There are 2 x 100% weigh hoppers at the bottom of SBC silo.

HCL, HF, and SO_3all removed at nearly 100% with SO_2in range of 60 to 65%. Na_2SO_3formation is negligible.

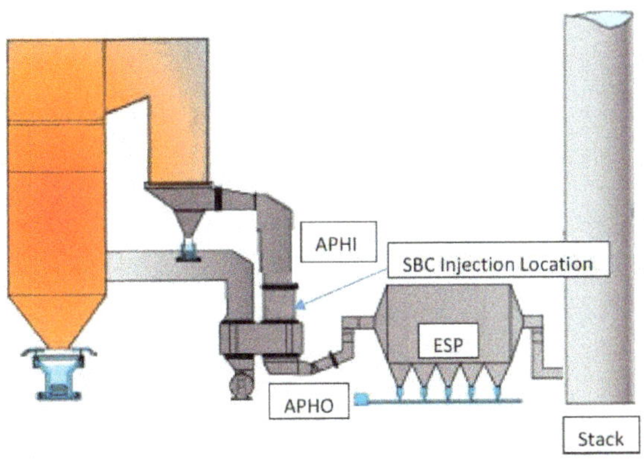

Fig - 1: Dry Sorbent Injection (DSI) System

CHAPTER FOUR

System Description of Wet FGD System

Wet FGD System can be sub divided in following sub systems:

1. **Flue Gas Path up to Absorber:**

Flue gas passes through the electrostatic precipitator (ESP) into Induced Draft Fans (IDFs). Downstream of the ID Fans, the common flue gas duct is branched into two paths. The first gas path leads into Wet FGD (WFGD) inlet gas duct through WFGD Inlet Damper feeding flue gas into the WFGD system for treatment. The second gas path directs flue gas through a bypass duct with a WFGD Bypass Damper thus directing flue gas into the stack without WFGD treatment. The WFGD inlet duct are provided with WFGD Inlet Guillotine Gate Damper to allow isolation of a WFGD while the second gas path is still in operation feeding into a common ductwork during WFGD Bypass and Boiler in full operation. Guillotine type flue gas dampers are provided upstream and downstream of each booster fan for isolating the booster fans. One bi-planar damper (along with seal air system) is provided on each bypass duct (existing duct) for allowing flue gas bypass operation to existing stack.

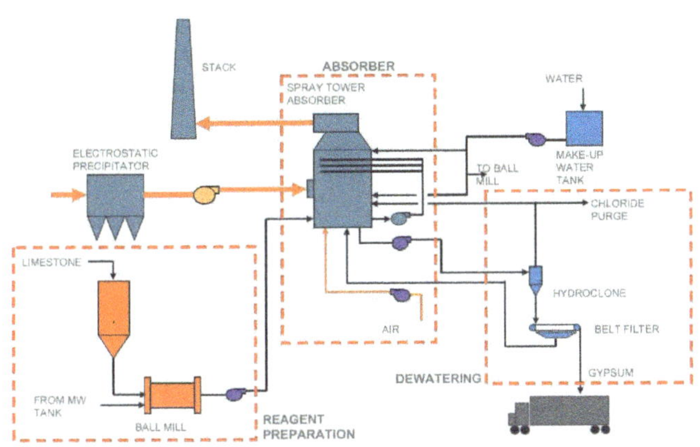

Process Flow Diagram of typical Wet FGD System

In the WFGD path, Flue gas from IDFs is introduced to Boost-Up Fans (BUFs) of FGD system. Required pressure compensation in flue gas due to installation of FGD is met by BUF, which then flows into the Absorber. Two booster fans per unit are provided to supply untreated flue gas to the absorber inlet flue gas duct. The boost up fans are generally rated to overcome the pressure drop in the inlet duct, Absorber and outlet ducting to wet stack including provision of pressure drop for future SCR installation and suitable margins as per specification requirement.

2. **Absorber System:**

The absorber consists of a counter current spray tower with gas distribution tray and an integrated reaction tank at the bottom. In the Absorber, the flue gas is cooled to its adiabatic saturation temperature by contact with recycle slurry, as the acid gases are absorbed. The flue gas flows upward from the bottom contacting with the sprayed slurry sent from the Slurry Recirculation Pumps. The flue gas enters the lower region of the absorber at a velocity and inlet angle calculated to minimize disturbance within the absorber.

$SO_2$and other pollutants are removed as the flue gas flows upwards through the spray zone. The spray zone is where the flue gas containing the $SO_2$is thoroughly contacted with the recirculated slurry spray in order to remove the desired amount of the SO_2. Thorough contact between the flue gas and the slurry droplets is necessary to achieve high efficiencies. The $SO_2$is removed through the absorption process and within the slurry droplets, the following reactions take place:

- SO_2in the gas near the surface of the recirculated slurry droplet is rapidly absorbed through the surface of the droplet forming HSO_3^-
- The HSO_3^-oxidizes to $SO_4^{2-}$by reaction with oxygen supplied by air introduced into the recirculation tank, referred to as **forced oxidation**.
- The calcium in the slurry pumped to the spray zone reacts with the $SO_4^{2-}$to form gypsum, i.e. $CaSO_4.2H_2O$.
- As the slurry is recirculated, the droplets leaving the spray zone are supersaturated with dissolved gypsum. Upon entering the large recirculation tank, the solution

de-supersaturates, the reactions go to completion, and the gypsum crystallizes out upon other gypsum particles held in suspension.

As the gas progresses upward through the spray zone, fresh recirculated slurry is introduced at each spray level to achieve the highest SO_2removal efficiency possible from the flue gas containing an ever-decreasing bulk SO_2 concentration. A fine droplet spray is delivered to the spray zone of the absorber through dual-directional, wide-angle, hollow cone spray nozzles, which are arranged on spray headers to provide complete coverage of the absorber tower cross-sectional area. The spray nozzles are supplied with low-pressure slurry by the recirculation pumps, one pump per spray level. The nozzle pressure is sufficient to generate small droplets and ensure uniform flow nozzle-to-nozzle, while not over-consuming power. The slurry is sprayed in the absorber through absorber slurry spray nozzles that are generally arranged in 3 separate spray stages. The absorber slurry is recycled with recirculation pumps (of identical type) from the lower part of the absorber to the spray nozzles in each spray level. The nozzles are fully drained by gravity. A controlled flow of the limestone slurry is fed into the absorber. Liquid droplets are collected from the flue gas when it passes through the mist eliminators. The gas is scrubbed with the recirculating gypsum / limestone slurry.

The recirculation tank (cylindrical and integrated as single unit with absorber having uniform diameter) is properly sized and designed to perform following important process functions:

- Mixing and dissolving the limestone,

- Oxidation of the dissolved HSO_3^- to SO_4^{2-},
- Providing sufficient residence time for the chemical reactions to go to completion,
- Providing a solid particles inventory for crystallization sites,
- Avoiding scale,
- Providing sufficient quantity of slurry to stabilize the process and
- Providing adequate recycle pump suction head.

Ambient air is pressurized and supplied to the absorber at the level of the agitators, deep within the slurry, by the oxidation air blowers, usually located near the absorber. The pressurized air is piped to each agitator through a ring header around the absorber. This ring header is arranged above the slurry level in the absorber to prevent slurry from flowing backward to the blowers during both normal operation and when the air blowers are off. The oxidation air supplied from oxidation air blowers is atomized into a large quantity of minute bubbles by means of shearing force given by the rotation of propeller of oxidation agitators and ejected towards the center of the absorber reaction tank, resulting in excellent oxidation efficiency.

The air exiting the blowers is hot due to the heat of compression, usually in excess of 95°C. If allowed to enter the absorber slurry directly, this hot air can create a wet-dry zone at the end of each air injection lance. The hot air would evaporate slurry and leave deposits of slurry solids on the lance, ultimately blocking airflow. To avoid that, water is sprayed into the hot air delivery pipe upstream of the injection lance. This water evaporates and cools the air to saturation conditions. At saturation conditions, the incoming air cannot evaporate any slurry and thus the wet-dry interface is avoided. This prevents plugging of the air lance.

Side entry agitators maintain the slurry in the absorber reaction tank in suspension. The same agitators work also as oxidation agitators. There are numerous side-entering agitators in the absorber, with the appropriate number and size selected to provide complete dispersion of air and suspension of solids.

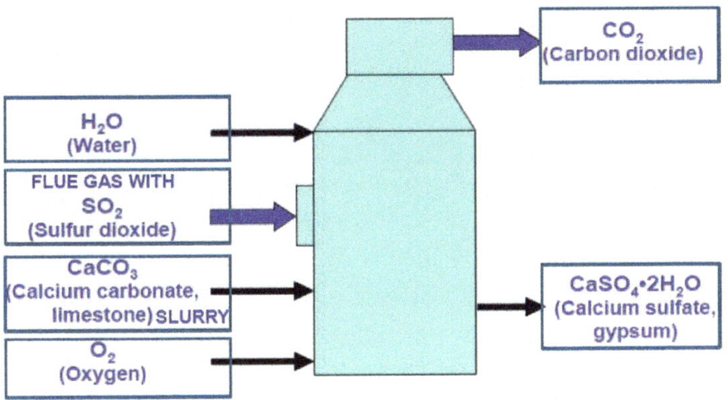

Reactions in Absorber

The process chemistries in absorber are as follows:

- Chemistry - Reaction Steps:

a. SO_2Absorption in ABSORBER

- $SO_2 + H_2O \rightleftharpoons H_2SO_3$
- $H_2SO_3 \rightleftharpoons H^+ + HSO_3^-$

- $HSO_3^- \rightleftharpoons H^+ + SO_3^{--}$

b. Dissolution Of Limestone: To Provide Alkalinity For Neutralization And Calcium Ion For Precipitation

- $CaCO_3 + 2\,H^+ \rightleftharpoons Ca^{++} + CO_2 + H_2O$

c. Oxidation Of Hydrogen Sulphites:

- $HSO_3^- + 0.5O_2 \rightleftharpoons SO_4^{--} + H^+$

d. Precipitation:

- $Ca^{++} + SO4^{--} + 2H_2O \rightleftharpoons CaSO_4.2H_2O$

The slurry is extracted from the absorber to the gypsum dewatering system by means of the gypsum bleed pumps. pH and density of this stream are monitored and pH level kept in range of 5.5 - 6. The gypsum slurry is removed from the absorber with gypsum bleed pump. The gypsum slurry return line is provided so that all gypsum slurry is returned to absorber without being fed to downstream gypsum dewatering system when slurry density is lower than set point. If the slurry density in the reaction tank is low, the feed valve to the primary hydrocyclone feed tank closes and the bypass valve opens routing the bleed back to the absorber. When the density builds back up, the feed valve to the primary hydrocyclone feed tank will open and the bypass valve will close allowing the slurry to be dewatered. This provides the control to hold the recycled slurry density at an average of 15% solids.

After the flue gas passes through the absorption section, it goes through three stages of mist eliminators for course and fine particle separation. The mist eliminator section of the absorber has been designed to provide:

- High efficiency removal with run-off provisions for the agglomerated drops to minimize re-entrainment.
- Low gas-side pressure drop.
- Access for inspections and maintenance of elements and washing nozzles.

Both sides of first two stages of mist eliminator and upstream side of last stage mist eliminator are intermittently washed with process water to avoid fouling with solids. The frequency and duration of the wash is based on the flue gas flow through the absorber. After passing through the three-stage mist eliminator, the treated flue gas goes to the wet stack and is released to atmosphere.

When the absorber is out of service, the slurry in the absorber can be extracted to the auxiliary absorbent tank directly via gypsum bleed pump or via absorber area sump pump. The slurry stored in the auxiliary absorbent tank will be returned to the absorber during normal operation after scheduled maintenance. Absorber drain valves allow the absorber to be fully emptied to the absorber area sump.

3. **Limestone System:**

Functions of this system includes Storage & Handling of limestone, wet ball mill system and Limestone slurry feed system. In a typical two unit's power plant, the limestone grinding system is common for both the units and provided with two separate streams (1W+1S) and each stream is suitable to handle the requirement of both units.

Limestone is the principal supplier of alkaline species necessary for SO2 absorption. It can be transported to plant by either Rail or Road. Unloading system depends on the mode of transportation. Limestone received to the plant by trucks, is unloaded by using the truck tipplers into the box feeders / bulk-receiving units. The capacity of a typical road fed Limestone handling system for 2x660 MW units power plant is 150 TPH. Generally specified Lump size of the limestone received at the project is (-) 250 mm. Crushing and screening system is provided to crush the limestone from (-) 250 mm to (-) 20 mm. The limestone is stored in a silo with opening(s) at the bottom. The limestone silo receives limestone from limestone handling system. Limestone handling system generally has magnetic separators, metal detectors, belt scales, sampling unit, belt protection switches, dust extraction system, service water system etc. For a typical 2x660 MW plant, Bulk storage silos (2 Nos.) suitable for 7 days of limestone requirement is generally provided, while Day Silos (2 Nos.) each suitable for one day requirement of Limestone is provided. The limestone discharged from the silo is led onto weigh belt feeders, which in turn feed the required quantity of limestone to grinding mill. The capacity of this feeder is designed to allow the maximum load operation of wet ball mill.

For any given limestone, the rate of dissolution is influenced by changes in the available surface area (grind size), absorber reaction tank size, and changes in the absorber pH. When a fine limestone grind is used, the rate of dissolution is maintained, even at higher absorber reaction tank pH levels. Because higher pH levels generally accompany an increase in the solution alkalinity, fine grinding of the limestone can increase SO_2removal at a constant stoichiometric ratio. Wet ball mill system consists of two streams, 1 in operation while the remaining stream being kept as standby. Each stream of wet ball mill system includes one (1) limestone weighing feeder, one (1) wet ball mill, one (1) mill slurry tank and agitator, two (2) mill slurry pumps, one (1) limestone slurry classifier, one (1) set of piping, valves and instruments.

The process water/ filtrate water line is connected to each wet ball mill for limestone slurry preparation. The wet ball mill has the closed circuit with the single loop classification by limestone slurry classifier (hydro cyclone). The limestone slurry leaving the wet ball mill enters the mill slurry tank. The Mill slurry tank receives the limestone slurry coming from the ball mill. The tanks are provided with necessary motorized agitator(s) to maintain the limestone water suspension (to avoid limestone deposits on the mill slurry tank). The limestone slurry from mill slurry tanks is transferred to classifier (hydro cyclone cluster) through mill slurry pumps. A part of coarse fraction is classified to the limestone slurry classifier underflow and returned to wet ball mill by gravity for further processing, and also can be returned to mill slurry tank when wet ball mill is stopped. The fine fraction is collected in limestone slurry classifier overflow and from there it goes by gravity to the limestone slurry storage tank as final product.

Limestone slurry tank is continuously agitated to prevent settling of solids. The limestone slurry is fed to the absorber by means of limestone slurry pumps. A return pipe line for the limestone slurry to limestone slurry storage tank secures an appropriate slurry velocity in piping irrespective of the load, and counteracts the deposition of solids on the pipe walls. The main limestone slurry feed line to the absorber is equipped with density meter, flow meter and control valve. The amount of the limestone slurry fed to the absorber is controlled by means of a control valve depending on the amount of $SO_2$and the pH value of the slurry in the absorber reaction tank. The slurry flow set point will be based on the SO_2removal set point and the average available CaCO3 in the limestone. Absorber slurry pH is maintained at minimum 5.5 to protect materials of construction and to prevent excessive amounts of limestone slurry from being added to the absorber. Bulk density of limestone for volume calculation is 1.4 T/m^3.

4. **Gypsum Dewatering System**

The gypsum slurry extracted from absorber by dedicated gypsum bleed pumps (1w + 1s) is fed to primary hydrocyclone (HC) of gypsum dewatering system located above vacuum belt filter. In hydrocyclones, the slurry is split into two streams, a low solid concentration stream of fine particles (dilute) known as the overflow and a high solid concentration stream of coarse crystals (concentrated) known as the underflow. The underflow of the HC flows by gravity to the feed box of the vacuum belt filter to produce cake of suitable moisture content and washing is provided to reduce chloride to the desired limits. The overflow is supplied to second stage hydrocyclone (HC) feed tank and partly to filtrate water tank.

From the secondary hydrocyclone feed tank (with top mounted agitator), the gypsum slurry is pumped to the secondary HC for further dewatering. Underflow from the secondary HC flows by gravity to the reclaim water tank. The reclaim water is pumped through reclaim water pumps to the Absorber reaction tank and the overflow from the secondary hydrocyclone flows to the hydrocyclone waste water tank. The waste water is pumped through waste water pumps to a Waste Water Treatment System. Purging wastewater from the dewatering system controls gypsum purity and chloride concentration level in FGD system.

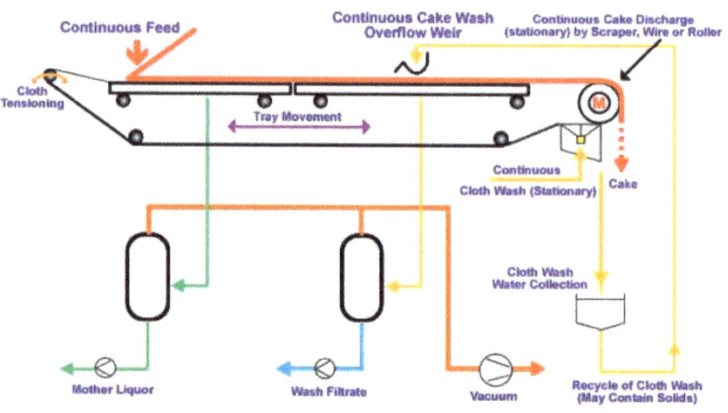

The concentrated slurry from the primary HC is further dewatered with the vacuum belt filter. The vacuum belt filter consists of a rubber belt, which carries an endless filter cloth and it slides over a vacuum box. The gypsum slurry from the primary HC underflow is distributed on the filter cloth and then the water in the slurry is separated from the gypsum by under pressure developed by vacuum pump. The separated water (filtrate) is collected to vacuum receiver. At the drive end, cake is discharged with the help of cake scraper and the filter cloth is washed with spray nozzles, The filtrate in the vacuum receiver is fed to the filtrate water tank by gravity.

5. **Gypsum Handling and Storage System:**

The filter cake builds up on the filter cloth as by-product gypsum and it is discharged through the discharge chute when the filter moves by the filter belt beyond the drive pulley. The gypsum cake falls from the chute to the Gypsum belt conveyor. Finally, gypsum is carried to the gypsum storage shed and stacked on the ground. Gypsum storage shed generally have a capacity for storage of produced gypsum for 7 days operation at FGD design condition. Density of gypsum for volume calculation is 0.9 T/m^3. Clearance for Truck movement from front end shall be minimum 3.1 m.

6. **Water System:**

The Water system includes Process water system, Filtrate water system, Equipment Cooling Water System, Waste water neutralisation system and Emergency Quench Water System.

CHAPTER FIVE

Cost of Wet FGD and Limestone & Gypsum Quantity

A. **Cost of Wet Limestone based FGD:**

In a brief review of the new MOEF&CC environmental rule, CEA published benchmark Base Cost for Wet Limestone based FGDs. This Base Cost is with new chimney and without GGH and does not include Taxes-Duties and Opportunity Cost for interconnection. As per CEA, the cost estimation given below is only indicative in nature and discovered through open competitive bidding for the projects already awarded:

S. No.	Capacity (MW)	Lakh per MW
1	195/210/250	45
2	300/330	43.5
3	500/525	40.5
4	600/660	37
5	800/830	30

The cost of Wet FGD system depends on many parameters including location of plant, greenfield vs brownfield plant, Unit size, space availability, range of SO_2removal, choice of corrosion protection lining, market forces etc. For a typical power plant (brownfield), it varies from 0.35 Cr/MW to 0.42 Cr/MW excluding taxes. For sub critical small size units, it may even be more than 0.43 Cr/MW. It also depends on the factor of safety selected by vendors. In a major contrast in civil works, one vendor spent nearly 1.5 times in civil works of FGD works of one stage as compared to other vendor, who is working in the vicinity in the FGD of second stage.

Some contractors prefer RCC over structure works and some prefer Structure works. In a typical plant with two units of 660 MW, where contractor prefers RCC, the civil work included RCC works of around 20500 Cum for Chimney & around 25000 Cum for General Civil works. Structure erection works is approx. 10500 MT & Equipment erection is approx. 1500 MT. In another typical plant with two units of 500 MW, where contractor prefers structural work, the civil work included RCC works of around 12500 Cum for Chimney & around 24000 Cum for General Civil works. Structure erection works is approx. 15000 MT & Equipment erection is approx 4500 MT.

Site condition like soil strata also plays a major role e.g. cost of FGD at one site, which has rocky strata & does not need piling, is around 0.36 Cr/MW, while for other site due to black cotton soil, piling was required and cost of FGD is 0.38 Cr/MW excluding taxes. Market forces also plays a major role as some vendors took orders with least possible profit margin to keep their companies floated in the market.

In case of Greenfield project, where Boiler chimney, absorber and wet chimney can be placed close to each other, the cost will be less compared to a brownfield project where they are far apart due to space constraints. In a typical Greenfield project, where Absorbers are kept near the Main plant chimney, there is no requirement of Boost up Fans. In addition, there will not be requirement of separate wet chimneys. However, the Main chimney to be lined by either titanium or C276. In such case, the cost of FGD package including work of chimney lining is around 0.23 Cr/MW excluding taxes. For a 275 m height chimney the typical cost of supply & erection of titanium lining is around 60 Cr excluding taxes. However, many developers are going for 150 m height chimney now. The Titanium or C276 lining is generally 2 mm thick lining on MS Flue can. Some contractors also prefer Borosilicate lining in the flue can. In some plants, Absorber tower also has C276 lining of 2 mm on MS Plates.

Since interconnection of chimney with absorber may result in loss of generation, this cost is called “Opportunity cost“. This can be reduced if this work is done during planned overhauling of units. A proper planning & coordination between Project Department, Planning Department and Maintenance Planning department can reduce this cost to Zero.

Operating Cost (OPEX) of FGD depends on Reagent cost, cost of Additional water consumption, O&M Manpower cost, APC of FGD, By-product handling and revenue earned through disposal of by-product etc. In a typical power plant of 500 / 660 MW, it varies between 4 to 6 Paise/unit. The Fixed Cost of FGD per unit of electricity varies a lot based on various selections. In a typical power plant of 2x660 MW, where FGD is installed after commissioning of units and separate Wet chimneys of 150 m installed for each unit, the fixed cost increased by around 20 Paise/unit due to FGD.

B. **Limestone Quality:**

There are approximately 15 parameters that influence O&M performance & Gypsum quality in FGD system. The key factor among these parameters influencing the performance is '**Quality of Limestone**'. In general, the improved purity of limestone results in:

- Improved purity of Gypsum and subsequently a better sale price of Gypsum.
- Decrease in limestone consumption.
- Decrease in APC of the FGD plant.
- Decrease in transportation cost of limestone/ton and Gypsum/ton.
- Decrease in maintenance cost of FGD plant. The maintenance cost of FGD plant normally varies between 2%-5% of FGD investment per year depending on the quality of the limestone apart from other factors.

In a typical FGD Contract, generally specified Limestone Purity in CaO % of mass is between 47% to 51%.

C. **Limestone Quantity Required for Wet Limestone based FGD:**

Limestone quantity required for Wet Limestone based FGD depends on 7 parameters of Flue gas at design point, which is entering into FGD, 5 different efficiencies of Absorber, purity of Limestone, quantity of BuF Seal Air and Stoichiometry (or Excess Ratio). Following values at design point are required to calculate Limestone quantity:

1. Gas flow at the FGD Inlet (Nm^3/Sec),
2. Moisture in Flue gas (% by Vol.),
3. SO_2 at Inlet (mg/Nm^3-wet),
4. Dust Quantity (mg/Nm^3),
5. HCl concentration (dry basis, ppm-d),
6. HF concentration (dry basis, ppm-d),
7. SO_3Concentration (dry basis, Nm^3/hr)
8. SO_2removal efficiency in absorber
9. HCl removal efficiency in absorber
10. HF removal efficiency in absorber
11. SO_3removal efficiency in absorber
12. Purity of Limestone
13. Stoichiometry (or Excess Ratio)

Based on above parameters Limestone quantity can be calculated with the help of chemical reaction equation in absorber. Stoichiometry (or Excess Ratio) is used for SO_3Capture & additional Design considerations. It is a proprietary value of vendor and varies based on design of Absorber. In a typical wet FGD, it can vary from 3 to 5% based on design of Absorber. For a typical 2x660 MW plant FGD, the quantity of limestone required for the plant is in range of 20 to 25 TPH.

D. Gypsum Quantity Required for Wet Limestone based FGD:

With the help of parameters used in calculating Limestone and chemical reaction equation in absorber, Gypsum produced can be calculated. For a typical 2x660 MW plant FGD, the quantity of gypsum produced at design point for the plant is in range of 34 to 40 TPH.

CHAPTER SIX

Civil Works

A. Geo Technical Investigation

Geotechnical investigation is carried out to obtain information about engineering properties of sub-surface soil, rock and water conditions around a site to finalize the foundationsystem for proposed structures.

Geotechnical investigation can be broadly classified into two categories i.e. field tests and laboratory work. Geophysical investigation is also conducted along with the field tests to obtain various physical properties like shear wave velocity, electrical resistivity etc. Geophysical investigations are also used as confirmatory tests for the geotechnical investigations.

The most important field test of any geotechnical investigation is standard penetration test. This test is being done to get information about the standard penetration resistance value i.e. 'N' value of soil. This test also enables us to get a soil sample at a desired depth to be used for laboratory testing. In case of rock, this test is being used to get information about core recovery and RQD of rock and also to obtain rock core samples for laboratory testing. Boring in soil and drilling in rock is conducted using rotary drilling rigs and hydraulic rigs. Depth of Investigation below ground level is decided upon the loads coming on the structures and also importance of structure. Number of boreholes in a particular area depends on the variation in the soil strata and also importance of the structures which is coming over it. In SPT test, borehole diameter is 150 mm in soil and 76 mm in rock. The Standard Penetration Test (SPT) is conducted inside exploratory boreholes to determine penetration resistance of soil. SPT is carried out as per IS: 2131 – 1981. The sampler used for SPT test is called split spoon sampler. The split spoon sampler resting on the bottom of the borehole is allowed to sink under its own weight. The drive assembly consists of a driving head and a 63.5 Kg weight with 75 cm free fall. The number of blows required to drive each 15 cm penetration is recorded. The blows required to penetrate the initial 15 cm of the split spoon for seating the sampler is ignored due to the possible presence of loose materials of cuttings from the boring operation. The cumulative number of blows required to penetrate the balance 30cm of the 45cm penetration is termed as penetration resistance – N value. The N values are presented on the soil profile for each borehole. Disturbed samples were collected from the split spoon after conducting SPT. Undisturbed soil samples were also collected for laboratory testing by attaching 75mm dia thin walled 'Shelby' tubes in accordance with IS 2132:1986.

There are number of other field test conducted during Geo Technical Investigation e.g. Standard Cone Penetration Test, Dynamic Cone Penetration Test, Seismic Refraction Test, Electrical Resistivity Test, Trial Pits etc. There are number of Lab tests also conducted for Geo Technical Investigation e.g. Natural Moisture Content Test, Grain Size Analysis, Hydrometer Analysis, Specific Gravity Test, triaxial shear test, consolidation test etc. These test helps in finding out the index as well as engineering properties of soil. The Strength Parameters i.e. Cohesion Stress (C) & Friction Angle (ø) is obtained from triaxial shear tests.

ζ = Shear stress of soil = C + σ tan ø

Where σ = Vertical stress.

In case of Rocks, Rock Quality Designation (RQD) is a Rough measure of the Degree of jointing or fractures in a rock mass & is used in estimating support of rock tunnels.

Based on the above mentioned field test and laboratory tests, geotechnical report is prepared which consists of various properties of soil prevailing at site and also the recommendations for foundation system for the various structures considering prevailing soil conditions.

B. **Open Foundation vs Piling:**

There are two types of foundations – Shallow (Footing) & Deep (Pile). Based upon the structure loads type of foundation system decided. In case of shallow foundations, each footing takes the concentrated load of the column and spreads it out over a large area, so that the actual weight on the soil does not exceed the safe bearing capacity of the soil. In design of shallow foundations, allowable bearing pressure is calculated considering shear as well as settlement criteria. For shallow foundations Foundation level is decided based on load bearing capacity.

A deep foundation is a type of foundation that transfers building loads to the earth farther down from the surface than a shallow foundation does to a subsurface layer or a range of depths. A pile or piling is a vertical structural element of a deep foundation, driven or drilled deep into the ground at the building site.

Pile foundations can take higher loads than footings. A pile is basically a long cylinder of a strong material such as concrete that is pushed into the ground so that structures can be supported on top of it. In deep foundations, pile capacities and pile length are worked out in accordance with IS 2904 Part-1/Sec-4: 1984. Each pile resists load by a combination of end bearing and friction. For Pile foundation, level is decided based on sum of end Load bearing capacity & Skin Friction.

C. **Piling Process:**

Piling works by inserting large amounts of wood, steel or concrete into the soil of the ground. The deep insertion of these elements ensures a sturdier base for the construction project to take place. In construction, they support buildings with weak soil and are driven into the ground by hammering.

There are two main types of pile, these are replacement and displacement. Replacement piles are put into holes or augured out of the earth to replace it. Displacement piles are pre-formed and driven into the ground, displacing the earth they are driven through.

Bored pile, also called drilled shaft, is a type of reinforced-concrete foundation that supports structures with heavy vertical loads. A bored pile is a cast-in-place concrete pile, meaning the pile is cast on the construction site. This differs from other concrete pile foundations, like spun pile and reinforced concrete square pile foundations, which use precast concrete piles.

In FGDs where piling is required, generally Bored Cast-In-Situ piling is done. The following basic machinery and equipment shall be utilized for the construction bored piles:

a. Service Crane
b. Self-Erecting Rotary Hydraulic Piling Rig
c. Vibrator
d. Wheel loader
e. Other complementary Drilling Tools and accessories (Casing, tremie pipe, auger, bucket, Bentonite Tanks, Circulation Pumps, Survey equipment, etc.)

Piling process is as follows:

1. **Drilling:**

a. Once the temporary casing has been installed, drilling of the pile are carried out by Self-Erecting Rotary Hydraulic Piling Rig with reverse mud circulation.
b. While drilling in the temporary casing, bentonite slurry of optimal density and viscosity is mixed in a mixer, installed on the site, and poured inside the hole stirring by an auger to provide the required support and protection to the sides of the borehole. The bentonite slurry shall be maintained up to top of casing pipe during drilling/boring operations & till the pile is concreted. The slurry shall be under constant circulation till start of concreting.
c. Drilling tools/bucket, Auger removes the soil inside the hole and deepens the bore hole. The drilling tool when filled up with the soil is lifted up and the spoil is dumped outside. The whole process continues till the desired stratum or depth of the hole is achieved.

2. **Reinforcement Installation:**

The readymade reinforcement cage, fabricated according to the design requirement and specifications, is slowly and carefully lowered into the hole, and centralized by means of roller spacer blocks, which are located along the cage periphery. Cover block spacing shall not be more than 1.5 m c/c along the axis of the pile and minimum three cover block shall be provided along circumferential direction. The installation of reinforcement is performed by using crawled/mobile crane with proper lifting capacity.

3. **Tremie Pipe Installation:**

The tremie pipe with funnel shaped hopper is placed in position at the top of casing to transport the concrete to the base of the pile.

4. **Concrete Placement:**

Concreting of the pile is done using a tremie pipe using high slump (150 to 180 mm) of concrete as allowed by the specifications / mix design. The time interval between the completion of boring and start of placing of concrete in pile bore shall not exceed 6 hours. Concrete is poured directly from the transit mixer into the tremie pipe or through a concrete pump. Concrete is continuously poured throughout the whole placement process to ensure a smooth operation. The top of concrete in pile as cast shall be above the cut-off level by 1.0m (min) to remove all laitance and weak concrete and to ensure good concrete at cut-off level.

5. **Trimming Of Piles Heads:**

The cutting or trimming of the excess concrete, also called pile chipping, will be done after the concrete has reached its initial set. Pile heads shall be chipped off to the cut-off levels until the sound concrete is exposed.

Pile Integrity Testing (PIT) is a Non-Destructive integrity test method for foundation piles. The method evaluates continuity of the pile shaft and provides information on any potential defects due to honeycombs, necking (cross-section reduction), potential bulbs, sudden changes in soil stratum, concrete quality in terms of wave speed etc. It is known as "Low Strain" method since it requires the impact of only a small hand-held hammer and the resultant strains are of extremely low magnitude. The test procedure is standardized as per ASTM D5882 and forms part of various specifications and code provisions worldwide. The testing shall be conducted at least 7 days after pile concreting.

D. **Wellpoint Dewatering:**

Dewatering means "the separation of water from the soil". The purpose is to control the surface and subsurface hydrologic environment in such a way as to permit the structure to be constructed "in the dry." This increases stability of excavation slopes and side-hill fills. Wellpoint dewatering is a process where groundwater levels are lowered enough to create a stable working environment. A wellpoint dewatering system consists of a series of shallow wells, known as wellpoints, which are installed at a pre-determined depth and appropriate spacing around an excavation. These wellpoints are connected to a main header pipe through riser pipes and are pumped out of the ground with a high-efficiency water pump.

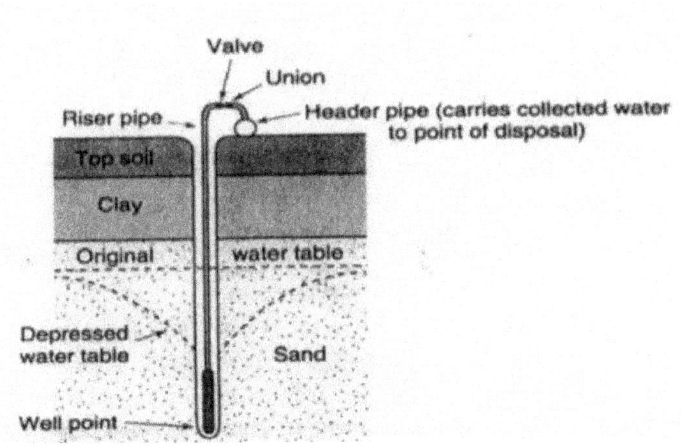

Advantages of this system are as follows:

- Rapid Installation
- Simple & cheaper equipment
- Water is filtered & carries little or no soil particles.

This system is generally used till 6 m depth below pump level as beyond that excessive air may be drawn into the system, resulting in loss in pump efficiency.

E. **Chimney:**

Concrete chimneys can be designed and constructed using one of two methods: slipform or jumpform. Slipform construction is suitable for very tall chimneys or chimneys with extremely large diameters, and for projects with tight deadlines to meet. Jumpform is based on more conventional concrete formwork techniques, to build the windshield in incremental stages.

1. **Slipping by Slip Form:**

Slip form is a special purpose formwork system used in construction of chimneys. This system controls the thickness of wall, radius of chimney at different heights and tapering of inside & outside surface of chimney according to the pre calculated design of chimney. This system carries the load of working persons, its components, shuttering, material etc. along with it by a hydraulic system of jacks, which are operated by a hydraulic power pack. The system keeps moving up and concrete keeps going continuously up to desired level without any stoppage. Yokes are suspended from the spider beams which keep on traveling radially inward as the work progress and give necessary taper to the chimney. These yoke legs carry the slip form circular shuttering system, which act as a shell mould and the thickness of the shell is controlled by the yoke beams, which connect the inner and outer yoke legs. The pre-designed walers control the radius of curvature of shell.

This system consists of fabricated spider beams spread radially outward from the center ring, equalling to the number of yokes are connected circumferentially by ribs form a basic platform at the top of the rising chimney. Wooden planks for movement of the concreting staff and engineers cover the top of system. This complete platform along with yoke legs & shuttering system remains suspended and takes the support from jack rods 32mm diameter, which are embedded in the chimney shell by means of hydraulic jacks, which are fitted with unidirectional grippers or catch.

i. **Slipform Erection Advantages Vs Disadvantages:**

- It offers the advantages of speed, safe work environment for workers, ability to produce a monolithic structure, reduced crane time and economy of operation.
- Due to continuous concrete pouring, it produces better concrete joints, superior finish & watertight structures.
- It can be used to construct tapered structures involving changing diameter & thickness in walls.
- High production rates can be achieved although careful planning is critical. The rate of climb is regulated to ensure that the concrete is self-supporting on emerging yet not so slow that the concrete hardens and binds on the forms. There is virtually no limit to the height and size of a structure that can be slipformed.
- The slipform operation can be stopped and resumed at will, to suit the contractor's schedule. Slipform operations can be suspended for the weekend or during parts of the day as dictated by external factors.
- The disadvantages are the high cost of the initial set-up, the need for specialist expertise & equipment and minimal flexibility for changes once slipform concrete has commenced.

ii. **Slipform System:**

Slipform System can be categorized into four sub systems:

a. Shuttering system
b. Mechanical control system
c. Hydraulic control system

d. Material handling system

Based on the size of chimney & site-specific parameters, various parts of system will change in number and capacity. For a typical 660 MW Unit, where a 150 m chimney is constructed, the system is explained below-

a. **Shuttering system:**

The function of shuttering system is to take care of shape of chimney and load of persons & material on it. After completing erection of Mainframe the 6 Nos. of wing beams shall be erected one by one and properly connected to centre frame at an angle of 60° between them.

After the erection of all 6 Nos. wing beams & connecting it to the center frame with all care of dimension and adequate checking, the spider beams shall be erected one by one and getting connected with ring beams at an angle of 10° in between them. Adopting the same sequence all the 30 Nos. spider beams shall be completed.

In a typical shuttering system, the spider beams are made out of ISMC 200 channels (2 nos. each). There is a gap of 100mm provided in the spider beams assembly to facilitate sliding of yoke legs, while reducing the radius.

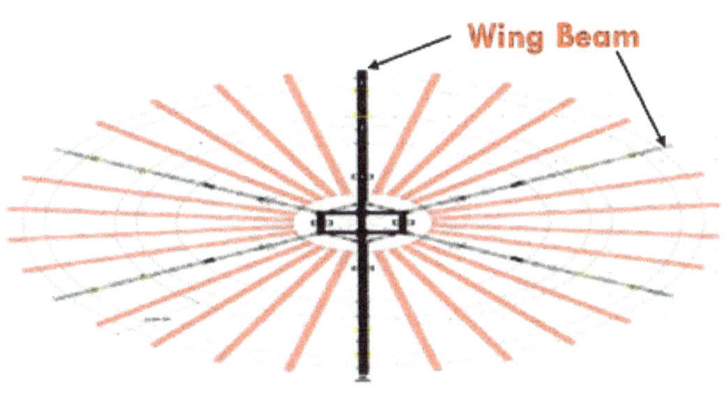
Wing Beam

Truss
(6 Nos.)
Main Hopper
for RCC
Top Deck
Middle
Deck
Lower
Waller
Lower/ Mason
Deck
Handrail

Nomenclature

Yoke Assembly:

The yoke assembly consists of one inside and outside yoke leg, each connected with two sets of channels otherwise known as yoke beams. The functions of yoke assembly are:

- To transfer the lifting force of jacks to the shutters, top deck, working deck and hanging scaffold.
- To support the top deck, working deck, hanging scaffold and shutter assembly while the jacks are fixed in position.

- Shell thickness Screw fixed with inner & outer yoke leg and Radius Screw fixed with inner yoke leg & Wing Beam/ Spider Beam.
- All the yoke legs kept in position with shuttering by adjusting the radius screw, which has been provided for the adjustment of radius at different elevations. Simultaneously, shell thickness Screw shall be operated to maintain the thickness of shell.
- The shutter assembly consists of shutters, waler and intermediate form supports. Shutters and walers retain the shape of structures to be slip formed.
- Cover block (50 mm) ensure that no reinforcement exposed outside RCC.

b. **Mechanical control system:**

- The main function of mechanical control system is to control the inner radius of chimney, wall thickness of chimney, inner and outer diameter of chimney and twisting of slip form.
- In a 36 yoke leg system there are 36 Radius screws (3 mm pitch) fitted each on inner yoke leg and spider or wing beam. When all the radius screws are given one revolution, the inner diameter of chimney gets reduced by 6mm.
- Spindles (2 mm pitch) control the inner and outer circumference of chimney. 120 inside spindles (60 left & 60 right threaded) are fitted along the circumference of inside diameter of chimney and 120 outside spindles (60 left & 60 right threaded) are fitted along the outer circumference of chimney.

- The function of horizontal turnbuckles is to reduce the circumference of shutter.

Wall Thickness Screw:

- This is also a special purpose screw of 2mm pitch, which controls thickness of chimney wall.
- There are 72 such screws fitted in slipform system, 36 nos. on inner yoke legs, upper yoke beam and 36 noson outer yoke leg, lower yoke beam are fitted.
- One set (2 Nos.) of wall thickness screw is provided for each yoke sets. The function of wall thickness screw is to reduce the wall thickness of the structure.

c. **Hydraulic Control System**

- Main functions of hydraulic control system are lifting of slipform, controlling inner and outer circumference and extraction of jack rods.

- Power pack is main part of hydraulic system, this is fitted with two hydraulic pumps and two motors to generate a pressure of 110 bars to operate different type of jacks fitted in hydraulic system.
- These are special purpose single acting, spring return jacks for lifting whole slipform. 6 Ton jack consists of one upper catch (top gripper) and one lower catch (bottom gripper) which grips the 32mm diameter jack rod, which is embedded in the concrete and climbs on it. The maximum stroke of jack is 50mm, bore diameter of cylinder 110mm, piston rod O.D. 50mm & I.D. 35mm. The working pressure of jack is 80 bars.
- There are 42 Jacks.
- Jack rods support the slip form assembly. The jack rod transfers the load of slip form assembly to ground/ wall. The entire load of whole slipform comes on these rods and jacks grip these rods and climb on it. The jack rods are housed inside a tapered sleeve tube. The tapered sleeve prevents climbing rod in contact with fresh concrete.
- These are round rods of EN8C approx. 3m length threaded on both ends, so that they can be joined together by means of suitable threaded studs.
- The jack rod will be extracted at convenient level and the holes created in the concrete will be grouted with cement slurry.

d. **Material Handling System:**

- The main function of material handling system in slipform is to transport concrete, work force, reinforcement rods & other material from ground level to top of slipform.
- Main components of this system are: Concrete winch, Material Winch, Passenger winch, Pulleys, Concrete bucket & trolleys. Concrete pump also used up to 12m at some places.
- Concrete trolleys are used to take concrete from concrete hoper to chimney walls through the MS funnel

and elephant hose on the top of slipform system.

2. **Flue can erection:**

Flues are fabricated in circular segments (cylinder) and erected from top to bottom. A construction opening is provided in chimney at bottom for transportation of segments inside chimney and erection. For convenience in fabrication, handling, transportation and erection the length of the flue 'CAN' is limited to the height of construction opening. The cans are to be classified as typical flue CANs, support cum restraint flue CANs, restraint flue CANs and S.S. flue CANs.

Typical flue CAN has stiffener angle at top and bottom with outstanding legs in horizontal plane serving as flanges for bolted connection. Support cum restraint flue CAN (Special CAN) is provided at the top of each unit of flue between expansion joints. This special CAN supports the total weight of this particular unit and transfer the load to the support beams through four brackets. This CAN also accommodate restraint buffers for the top restraint bracket of the unit. At the end of this CAN, where the bracket / restraint buffers are provided, stiffness of CAN is increased by providing stiffeners and local higher thickness for CAN. Flange connection at the end of the CANs as well as stiffeners are provided similar to typical flue CANs. It is very important to fabricate the CANs with stiffeners, brackets at exact designed locations and same shall be checked before shifting to chimney for erection.

The exposed surface of top CAN, above roof slab, shall have a box shaped stiffener. External exposed surface of this CAN shall be wrapped with 2 mm thick titanium/ C276 sheet over insulation. The supporting / restraining arrangements of the flue/duct shall be such that the movement of the flue longitudinally or circumferentially is not restrained.

Erection Methodology:

- All the columns, beams and bracing fabricated as per drawing erected over the top of roof slab by means of bolts or inserts embedded during casting. All those lifting Beams & Bracings are lifted from Ground level with the help of winches.
- After the erection of lifting beams, the mounting of jacks is done over the frames as per drawing. The jacks

are aligned properly in the position. In a typical 150m chimney, the diamond formation shall be worked out placing 2 Nos 20 MT jacks over the lifting beam. At the centre of the Jacks 1 no. anchor device consisting of top anchor and bottom anchors shall be placed. Alongside of this arrangement same arrangement with 2 more jacks will be done to accommodate one more strand rope.

- These 4 jacks for lifting 2 strands arrangement shall be repeated at all the 4 corners of the flue opening on the roof slab. This means that one segment of flue can shall be erected by means of 8 nos. of ropes i.e. 16 nos. Jacks shall be used for erection of flue can segments.
- 90 lbs rails of required length will lead from centre line of flue to 30m outside the chimney to facilitate the transportation of CAN over the trolley from outside of chimney to the location.
- Anchor the HT strands coming from the lifting jack and anchor barrels to the lifting bracket, attached to the topmost CAN 'C1'.
- Lift the CAN 'C1' to a height just sufficient to accommodate next CAN 'C2' under it.
- Bring CAN 'C2' inside the chimney, align and connect CAN 'C1' & 'C2' by bolting/welding as per approved drawing & specifications. Inside welding is done by circular Jhula suspended through a wire rope connected to power winch (say 3 MT).
- Flue can outside fit-up and bolting are done by a circular jhula suspended through chain pulleys and sling rope connected to lowest support platform (43.5 M in a typical 150 m chimney).
- Lift the assembly of CAN 'C1' & 'C2' to accommodate next CAN 'C3' under it. Repeat the above process. Rest the final assembly of CANs at the base.

- Remove the HT strands Anchored to CAN 'C1' and attach to the bracket on the lowest CAN.
- Lift the assembly of CANs up to the required elevation. Align the assembly so that the last Flue-Can can rest on the restraint platforms.
- Put the restraint brackets on the platform and carefully bolt the bracket assembly with the CAN assembly. In a typical 150 m chimney, there are typically four support platforms. Release the load once the assembly is checked by the quality team.
- Remove the lifting tackles from lowest CAN of assembly and lower down the HT strands to facilitate the lifting of next assembly.
- Repeat the above process for erection of complete Flue CAN.

3. **Borosilicate Lining**

Penetration of flue gases through cracks in the air space can cause acid attacks on brick liners, which can lead to mortar and concrete erosion. Structural and thermal stresses and stresses that are concentrated at corners can cause cracking in an independent brick liner. Years of use, acid condensation, and change in operation can cause the mortar and brick to soften, making the brick liner vulnerable to cracks or leaks. Scrubber operation, salt deposits and moisture penetration cause leaching, which may damage hood and interior platform alignments.

Lightweight borosilicate glass blocks are attached to the internal surface of power plant chimneys, stacks, flues, liners and ducts, using a durable, flexible adhesive to resist a number of challenging conditions. Borosilicate Lining system has extensively been used since more than a decade.

Acid Resistance Borosilicate Foam Glass blocks were designed to meet the operating conditions of Wet FGD. High Boron content ($B2O_3$: 10 -13%) makes it thermal shock resistance at sudden change in temperature of flue gas. High Silica Content (SiO_2 : 70 - 80%) makes it acid resistance to almost all acids/salts generated after reaction of flue gas in Absorber.

Borosilicate Blocks are Inorganic due to which it has indefinite storage life. Closed Cell structure makes it resistant and impermeable to water, acid gas and acid condensate even under positive pressure conditions. As no binders are used and the blocks are manufactured using Borosilicate Glass therefore it is not combustible.

High porosity gives it good insulation property and it has very low Thermal Conductivity. Borosilicate Glass raw material selected is of very low coefficient of linear thermal expansion. The light weight of borosilicate blocks is suitable for use in Chimneys without any support. Borosilicate lining system has long service life of 30 years or over even higher.

Anticorrosive Epoxy Primer is selected due to its excellent anticorrosion properties and it provides good adhesion to adhesive membrane. Anticorrosive urethane adhesive is selected as it is resistance to all the acids / salts generated in Wet FGD Flue gas. Elastomeric property of the adhesive makes it flexible for long run and it last for decades. The adhesives bond the borosilicate blocks very nicely to the substrate and it has excellent tensile and bond strength.

Globally borosilicate blocks are manufactured into big blocks of 600*500 mm or even more. Then these big blocks are sized into small blocks as per the requirement of the

Customer. Generally selected thickness of one block is 38 mm or 51 mm. Generally, the size of one block is 229 x 152 mm. Density of Borosilicate block is in range of 190-210 kg/m^3.

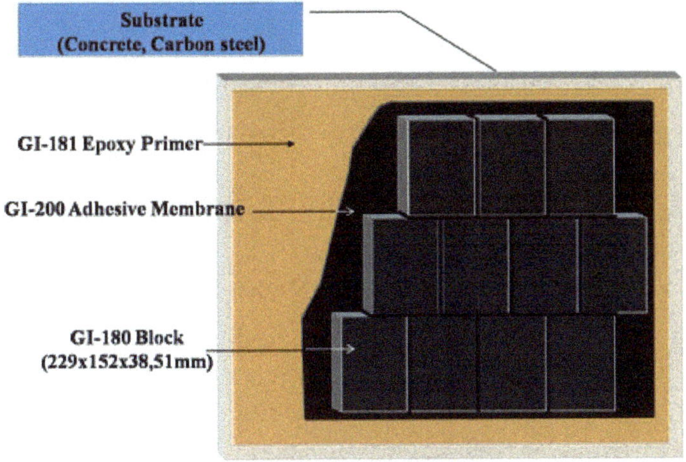

Typical Borosilicate Block Arrangement

CHAPTER SEVEN

ABSORBER

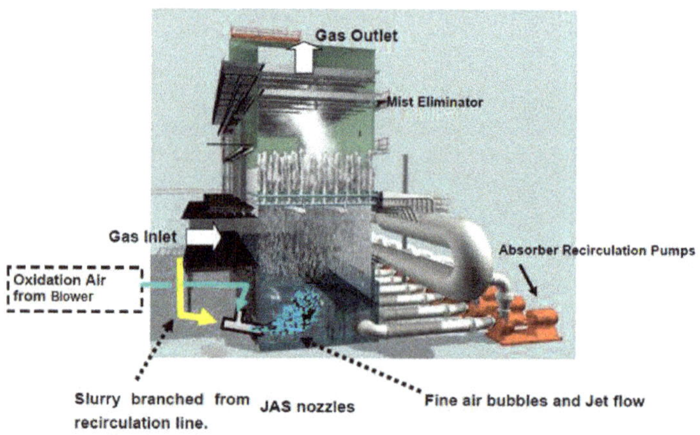

Typical Double Contact Flow Scrubber (DCFS) Absorber

Critical design features are built into the absorber to accommodate the relatively short residence time during which the SO_2in the incoming flue gas must make efficient contact with a complete surface area of available reagent in order to be efficiently absorbed. Each internal device within the absorber system is important to the overall performance and economy of operation. The absorber slurry system is a combination of several subsystems. These subsystems work together to maintain the absorber material balance, the absorber slurry chemistry (pH), the density (solids percentage), and the reaction tank liquid level. Absorber and its slurry recirculation system are designed for specified % removal of inlet SO_2at Design & Guarantee points.

Open spray tower with multiple spray levels and integrated forced oxidation tank.

Absorber Sizing Calculation:

Absorber is designed for a specified superficial flue gas velocity corresponding to the absorber outlet flue gas conditions. Different vendors select different values of it. Maximum acceptable superficial velocity through absorber corresponding to saturated gas conditions is also specified by Owner in tender document. It is generally in range of 3.5 to 4.5 m/s. Let's Assume it as A m/sec.

FGD Outlet Gas Flow rate at design point is also specified in a tender. It also depends on size of unit. Let's assume it as B m^3/sec.

Minimum Absorber vessel cross section area shall be A/B m^2.

Based on this width & length for rectangular absorber or diameter for Circular absorber vessel can be selected.

The design of the reaction tank ensures that sufficient tank volume is allowed for limestone dissolution, oxidation of sulphites and crystal growth of calcium sulphate (gypsum). Based on QFGDM's design practice and parameters specified in tender documents following can be calculated:

- Sizing of Absorber Wet Dry Interface
- Sizing of Recirculation Tank
- Sizing of Expansion & Spray Zone
- Sizing of Mist Eliminator Zone
- Sizing of Outlet Cone

As these data are highly vendor specific and needs permission of different vendors to share, these calculations are not included in this book. However, Author can be contacted for seeking help for these calculations.

Absorber Material:

The absorber is protected from the corrosive and erosive effects of the agents involved. Depending upon the agents, different parts of absorber have different material. Major material details are as follow:

1. Inlet Duct & Dampers:

Absorber inlet gas temperature is above acid dew point and is in range of 150°c. This can be taken care by Carbon Steel.

2. Inlet Wet/Dry Interface:

This interface is exposed to both the incoming dry hot flue gas and the absorber slurry sprays. At the wet/dry interface, it is necessary to install a solid Alloy 59 or C-276 of minimum 6 mm thickness.

3. Absorber vessel:

The tank is exposed to corrosion inducing environment. There is also abrasive wear due to solids "Sweeping" action due to agitator induced & recirculation pump suction-induced currents. The absorber shell be designed for pressure load, live load, piping forces and moments, hydrostatic load, wind & seismic loads. The tank and tower shall be provided with lining/ cladding/ wallpaper of Alloy 276/ Alloy 59 or better material on Carbon Steel. Similarly, internal column & Lower deck beams are made of carbon steel wrapped with lining/ cladding/ wallpaper of Alloy 276/ Alloy 59.

4. Spray Zone:

Multiple levels of headers with spray nozzles are used to provide complete cross-sectional coverage and to meet the stipulated guarantee and design requirement. All internal members shall be lined with Alloy 59/ 276 of specified thickness.

The spray headers shall be made of FRP or Carbon Steel with rubber lining or ceramic coated. The spray nozzle shall be of silicon carbide (SiC) or ceramic or equivalent.

5. Mist Eliminators:

Key issue is corrosive attack by sulphurous & sulfuric acid, resulting from the combination of wash water with the residual SO_2& SO_3in the clean gas. Generally, three stage chevron type Mist Eliminators made of polysulfone (PSU) or stainless steel shall be provided at the exit of the absorber.

Alloy C276:

Alloy C-276 is a solid solution strengthened nickel-molybdenum-chromium alloy with a small amount of tungsten. Alloy C-276 exhibits excellent corrosion resistance in a variety of harsh environments and media. Like many other nickel alloys, it is ductile, easily formed and welded. This alloy is used in most industrial settings where aggressive chemical environments are present and other alloys have failed. Alloy C-276 is one of the most universally corrosion resistant alloys available. Alloy C-276 Chemical Composition (%):

1	(Ni) Nickel	Remainder
2	(Mo) Molybdenum	15.0 to 17.0
3	(Cr) Chromium	14.5 to 16.5
4	(Fe) Iron	4.0 to 7.0
5	(W) Tungsten	3.0 to 4.5
6	(Co) Cobalt	2.5 max
7	(Mn) Manganese	1.0 max
8	(V) Vanadium	0.35 max
9	(Si) Silicon	0.08 max
10	(P) Phosphorus	0.04 max
11	(S) Sulfur	0.03 max
12	(C) Carbon	0.010 max

Courtesy: corrosionmaterials.com

Erection of Absorber:

There are many types of absorbers in the market. Based on shape, Absorbers can be rectangular or circular. The final shape changes the erection methodology of erection of absorber. In a circular absorber, first shell is erected and then structures from outside erected. In a rectangular absorber, first structures are installed and then plates erected taking support from structure members. Erection philosophy changes depending upon the type of absorber, shape of absorber, vendor expertise, resource availability etc. Plate by Plate & Ring method is generally used for circular absorber erection.

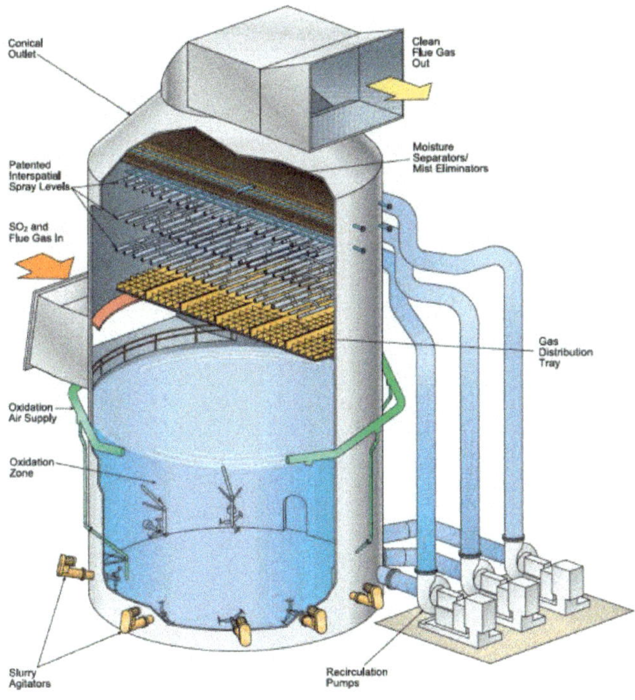

Following is the erection philosophy of Circular absorber:

1. Cladded plates shall be stacked in a way that each plate separated by suitable packing materials to avoid direct contact between CS portion and alloy portion.

2. For rolling of cladded plates Rolling machine with rubber lined roller or rubber roller can be used.
3. Dimensions of the plates after the rolling shall be checked with a template made of GI sheet or cardboard.
4. After rolling/bending, cladded plates are stacked (Vertical Stacking as well as horizontal) in such a way that they are separated by suitable packing materials to avoid direct contact of cladded (C276) portion with MS/CS portion of the plates.
5. Before starting the preassembly, identified area shall be developed for Crane/Hydra movement & assembly. Scaffolding towers of height 3 & 5 meter are prepared for the shell plate fit-up at ground level.
6. Tyre mounted pick n carry crane of required capacity used for the plate feeding during assembly of shell as well as duct.
7. After the fit up of shell course assembly, for checking flatness of the shell top, water level method of inspection shall be carried out and for checking verticality plumb method shall be used.
8. For duct opening portion assembly, dummy rolled plate or rolled channels/ angles shall be used to avoid buckling during lifting. The same is connected to the absorber shell with stitch weld.
9. Base plate fixing sequence:

Base Plate Fixing →Anchor Bolt Fixing→ Bottom Plate Fix→ Diagonal plate fixing

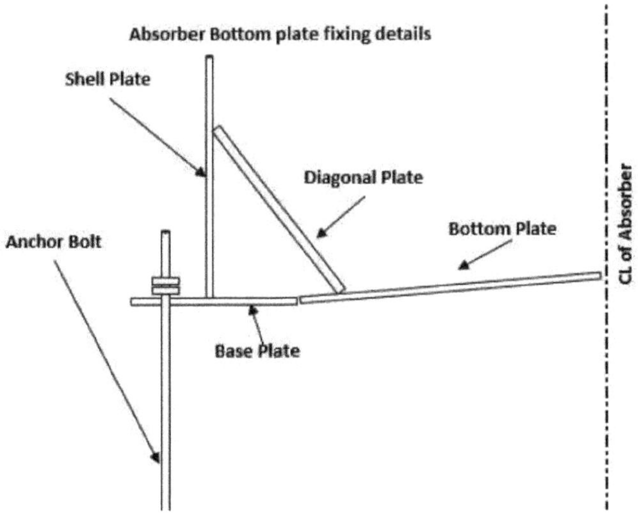

10. After the insertion of the bottom base plate, cladded portion of the base plate shall be covered by rubber mat to protect the C276 alloy metal from damage during the shell construction.
11. From 1stto 3rdshell, erection is generally done with plate by plate method and for Shell courses above that generally Ring method is used with the help of the 250 MT or equivalent capacity crawler crane. Jacking Method can also be used in place of using cranes.
12. Drain pipe shall be fixed to bottom plate before setting of the foundation.
13. Welding joint discrepancy of vertical direction & circumferential should met the design tolerances.
14. For the lifting of the assembled shell, lifting hook arrangement called octagonal spider beam arrangement

shall be provided to lift at 08 locations on the shell to avoid the ovality occurrence during lifting.

15. Absorber internals (Mist Eliminator Beams, Mist Eliminator, Spray Systems etc.) shall be erected after the shell course erection up to hood erection.
16. External stiffeners should be ensured before erection of inlet & outlet duct.
17. Internal erection sequence:

- Mist eliminator Bracket & Primary Beam erection
- Spray Header erection (1ststage to 3rdstage) (Bottom to Top)
- Primary & secondary beam of perforated tray
- Perforated Tray
- Agitators
- Erection of mist eliminator upper/lower

The mist eliminator is located in the absorber above the scrubbing zone and consists of three stages: the course, fine, and finest eliminator. The coarse eliminator is 1ststage eliminator and located bottom most location. The fine eliminator is 2ndstage eliminator and located at lower side of diamond shape. The finest eliminator is 3rdstage eliminator and located at upper side of diamond shape.

18. Beams are erected in bottom to top sequence. Support beams coming in centre are erected in a later stage. This is to facilitate movement of mist eliminator and spray header through centre of absorber.
19. Mist eliminator assembled on the ground before installation.
20. Winch is used for erection of spray headers.
21. Sprayer header is lifted by utilizing the beam of absorber upper part.
22. Site joint between spray header and spray pipe is connected with FRP adhesives.

CHAPTER EIGHT

CONTROL PHILOSOPHY

The FGD control system is based on remote automation philosophy. The FGD system control requires signals from the boiler/turbine control system. The Distributed Digital Control Monitoring and Information System (DDCMIS) ensures supervision, command, protection, and process control (regulation and automation). This system control also depends on envisaged equipment in FGD System. In case of FGD System for a new unit, Boost Up Fans (BuF) and separate Wet Chimney may not be required. In case of FGD System for an old unit, they may be required or not required depending upon space availability & layout. This chapter explains Control Philosophy of a FGD System where both Boost up Fans and separate Wet Chimney are envisaged for each unit.

A. **Control Systems:**

The FGD plant is designed for not to interfere on the boiler operation and to maintain the specified desulfurization performance, in spite of the boiler load-change by controlling the absorbent feed rate to the absorber. There are many major and minor control system in a FGD system. Major Control System are:

1. Flue Gas Flow Control
2. Limestone Slurry Feed Control
3. Absorber Level Control

Minor Control System are:

4. Absorber Slurry Density Control
5. Absorber Gas Inlet and Mist Eliminator Washing Control
6. FGD Make up Water Tank Level Control
7. Waste Water Flow Rate Control to FGD Waste Water Transfer Tank
8. Waste Water Flow Rate Control to Ash Slurry Sump
9. FGD Make up Water Flow Rate Control to Wet Ball Mill System
10. Gypsum Cake Thickness Control

All above controls are explained in detail below-

1. **Flue Gas Flow Control:**

When FGD is not in service, Bypass Damper will be completely OPEN and all the flue gas will be evacuated through Bypass Damper.

The flue gas from Induced Draft Fans (IDF) flows to the FGD is discharged to the wet stack. To avoid affecting the normal operation of the existing plants, FGD inlet pressure is to be controlled by means of the Boost Up Fan to keep the constant value, which is demanded by the functional set point of IDFs outlet pressure related operation load.

The Feed Forward control loop determines the required flue gas flow rate to the FGD which is calculated from the boiler air flow rate. The Feed Back control loop finely tunes the FGD inlet gas flow rate using the FGD inlet pressure control. Demand signal is generated and provided to Booster Fans Blade Pitch Actuators, to maintain the ID Fan common discharge duct pressure during flue

gas treatment operation.

ID Fan common discharge duct pressure increases when boiler load increases. The Booster Fan Blade Pitch controller respond to this increase in demand, which will increase the Booster Fan Blade Pitch Actuator, which consequently decreases IDF common discharge duct pressure. Bias adjustments are provided to balance the Booster Fan loads by monitoring fan motor current. When FGD is to be taken into service, Booster Fan will be started with minimum Blade Pitch opening.

During excessive furnace pressure conditions directional blocks on Booster Fan Blade Pitch controller is applied if used on the boiler ID Fans controller. During extremely low furnace pressure conditions, the Booster Fan-Blade Pitch Actuator will not allow to increase pitch movement and conversely during high pressure furnace conditions Booster Fan-Blade Pitch Actuator will not allow to decrease pitch movement.

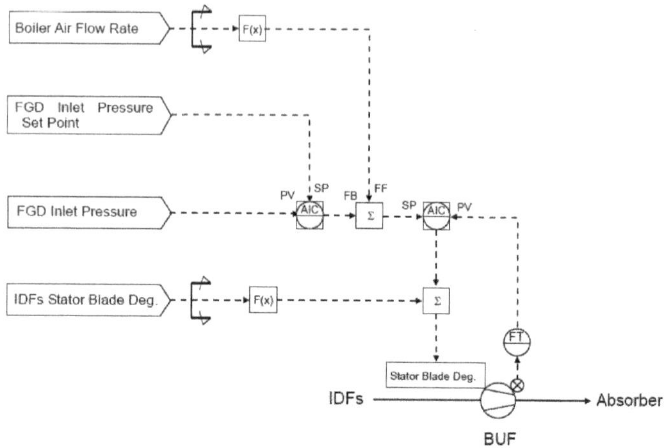

When flus gas path is not available (WFGD Bypass Damper is closed AND Booster Fan-A I/L Gate is closed AND Booster Fan-B I/L Gate is closed), the furnace will be pressurized and to eliminate this hazard, ID Fan should trip. If both BuF-A & B are trip, the WFGD plant will be bypassed (Bypass Damper will open automatically), However, in case when only one BF is trip, the operating BuF shall be operated in full capacity (single BuF flow) and remaining flow will be bypassed through existing stack.

2. **Limestone Slurry Feed Control:**

Limestone slurry is continuously supplied to the absorber to make up the reagent consumed in the absorber. The flow rate to the absorber is controlled by a Feed Forward and Feed Back control loop. The Feed Forward control loop determines the required limestone feed rate to the absorber by using the inlet sulfur load which is calculated from the FGD inlet gas flow rate and inlet SO_2concentration. The Feed Back control loop finely tunes the limestone feed rate using the pH control.

The total SO_2value is calculated by multiplying the BUF outlet gas flow rate and the SO_2concentration. The absorber slurry pH is calculated by averaging of two (2) absorber slurry pH measurements. The absorber slurry pH set value is programmed from the absorption quantity. Generally, pH set value is in range of 5.5 to 6.

The limestone slurry flow is calculated by multiplying the SO_2absorption quantity and the limestone excess ratio. Then it is to be divided by the limestone purity to calculate necessary limestone solid amount. The necessary limestone slurry feed amount is calculated by the density of limestone slurry.

To prevent deterioration of the FGD performance due to the absorber slurry pH decline, the calculated amount of limestone slurry based on boiler load change rate is added to the setting value.

If both the Limestone Slurry pumps are unavailable during absorber in operation and pH becomes less than a set value, say 4.5, then a request will be generated through an HMI indication and alarm for an operator action to activate WFGD Bypass condition.

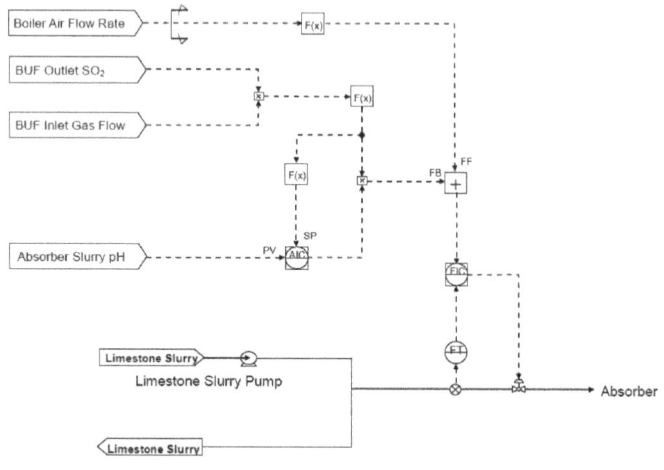

3. **Absorber Level Control:**

Gypsum slurry is discharged to the primary dewatering system from absorber and also water exits the absorber through evaporation, the level in the reaction tank gradually falls. The majority of the Absorber Process water will consist of a combination of fresh water, wash water from mist eliminator washing, filtrate water reclaimed from the primary and secondary dewatering operations. To compensate the water losses from the FGD system, FGD make-up water is continuously added to the absorber to balance this water loss.

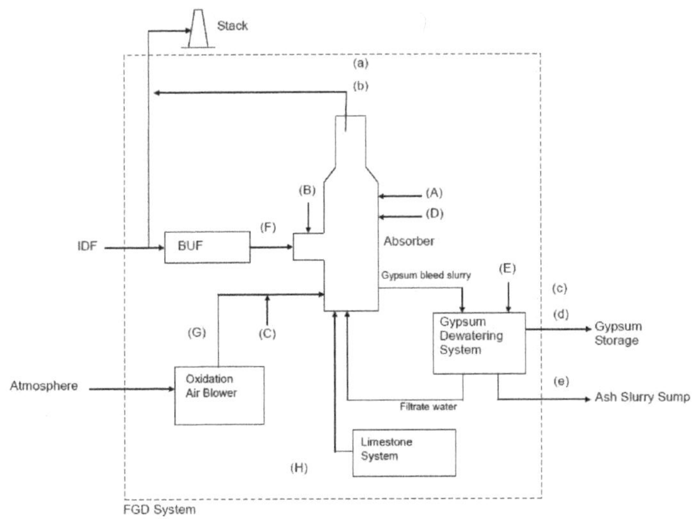

Water goes to the absorber by the following sources:

A. Mist eliminator wash water (The amount of mist eliminator wash water is determined by the boiler load)
B. Absorber gas inlet wash water
C. Oxidation air quenching water
D. Directly added water to absorber for level control
E. Gypsum dewatering system wash and seal water
F. Water vapour in inlet gas
G. Water vapour in oxidation air
H. Water in limestone slurry feed to absorber
A. The water in gypsum bleed slurry is returned to the absorber as the filtrate water

Water is lost from the absorber by the following mechanisms:

a. Water vaper in outlet gas (Water evaporation for cooling the flue gas : (a) - (F) - (G))
b. Mist carryover
c. Water in gypsum cake
d. Bound crystal hydration in gypsum
e. Waste water

Three (3) differential pressure instruments continuously monitor the absorber level. The process water is utilized as make-up water to maintain a level of the absorber reaction tank constant.

4. **Absorber Slurry Density Control:**

Gypsum in the absorber slurry is produced by chemical reaction between limestone and oxidized SO_2. The density in the reaction tank is controlled to maintain the correct residence time of the gypsum crystals growing in the reaction tank and to prevent scaling of the absorber internals. The density of the Absorber Recycle slurry is measured in the common discharge of the Gypsum Bleed Pumps.

Gypsum dewatering system shut-off valve will be opened or closed depending on the gypsum slurry density. This kind of control ensures that the density is kept about constant in the entire load range and corresponds to the solid content 18 to 20% (weight). When the density is higher than the set point value, the absorber slurry is fed to the Gypsum Dewatering System to reduce the absorber slurry density. On the other hand, when the density is lower than the set point value, the absorber slurry is fed to the return line to the absorber and there is no discharge to the Gypsum Dewatering System.

5. **Absorber Gas Inlet and Mist Eliminator Washing Control:**

The absorber gas inlet post is continuously washed to minimize corrosion and solid deposition. Each face of each stage has the different washing sequence interval depending on the location. The Mist Eliminator (ME) system consists of a three (3) stage Mist Eliminator with a washing system to remove solid deposition on the face of the elements. The automatic wash cycle is a predetermined sequence, cleaning one section at a time.

The Mist Eliminator Wash Pump is either a manually initiated operation by the WFGD Operator from the DDCMIS interface terminals or an automatically initiated operation by the DDCMIS as the result of start-up sequence operation. Basically, the washing sequence interval is determined by the boiler load. The frequency decreases as the boiler load decreases. In case of lower boiler load, the washing sequence interval is extended to keep the water mass balance.

A possible cause of FGD inlet pressure high is mist eliminator plugging. If the High FGD differential pressure alarm is activated, the operator should check the mist eliminator differential pressure. If the mist eliminator differential pressure is higher than the normal pressure drop at the design boiler load, the operator should start the mist eliminator washing sequence manually to clean the mist eliminators. However, if the mist eliminator differential pressure continues to rise to the value of High

Alarm, the operator needs to reduce the boiler load or stop the BUF and close the FGD inlet and outlet dampers and the FGD system should be taken into an outage to allow the inspection (and cleaning, if necessary) of the mist eliminators.

6. **FGD Make up Water Tank Level Control:**

The service water feed flow is controlled by the Process water tank level. When the level in the Process water tank is higher than the high set point value, the Make-up water valve will be closed and it will stay in closed position until the water level will reach the low set point level.

7. **Waste Water Flow Rate Control to FGD Waste Water Transfer Tank:**

Secondary stage Hydro Cyclone overflow is collected in FGD Waste Water Tank, which is neutralized with hydrated lime. Secondary stage HC feed is controlled by the level of secondary stage HC feed tank. If the level of secondary stage HC feed tank is lower than set point, secondary stage HC feed line is closed and recycled to secondary stage HC feed tank using minimum flow line of secondary stage HC feed pump.

8. **Waste Water Flow Rate Control to Ash Slurry Sump:**

FGD Waste Water is sent to Ash Slurry Sump by FGD Waste Water pump. If the level of FGD Waste Water tank is lower than set point, feed to FGD Waste Water is stopped by stopping the FGD Waste Water pump.

9. **FGD Make up Water Flow Rate Control to Wet Ball Mill System:**

Filtrate water or FGD process water is used for the limestone slurry preparation and the make-up water flow rate is controlled to keep the constant value which is demanded by the limestone slurry density at the outlet of the limestone mill slurry pump. The make-up water is fed to the limestone mill system in normal operation. There are two (2) lines of the make-up water. One line is connected to the inlet of the wet ball mill and the other is connected to the mill slurry tank. The make-up water flow rate to the wet ball mill is controlled to keep the constant value which is demanded by the functional set point of the limestone

feed rate to the wet ball mill. On the other hand, the make-up water flow rate to the mill slurry tank is controlled to keep the constant value which is demanded by the limestone slurry density.

10. **Gypsum Cake Thickness Control:**

In the deviation correction signal, which is programmed from the deviation of gypsum cake thickness set value and gypsum cake thickness signal, calculates and outputs the vacuum belt filter drive demanded by proportional and the integral action.

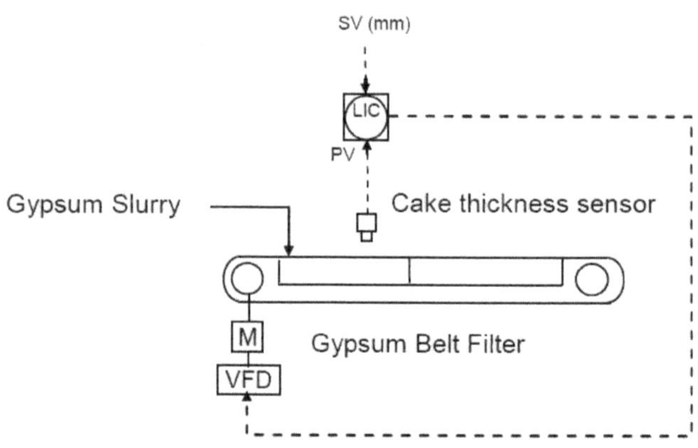

B. **Start-up of FGD Plant:**

Pre-conditions needed from Boiler/ Main plant for FGD Flue Gas system start-up are listed below:

a. BOILER MFT is reset / No BOILER Trip (*Signal from SG DDCMIS→FGD DDCMIS*)
b. BOILER LOAD is > Minimum Load (Prespecified)
c. ID FAN Outlet Pressure is ≥ 0 mm H_2O.
d. ID FAN Outlet Temperature is ≤ Prespecified temperature (typically 150°c)
e. ESP is ON.

C. **Control Philosophy of Boiler MFT:**

Separate DCS is envisaged for FGD. Signal exchange from Main boiler DCS to FGD DCS takes place. Whenever the Main Fuel Trip (MFT) is initiated in main boiler DCS, this signal is transmitted to FGD DCS also. After receiving MFT from FGD DCS, following changes takes place:

1. Emergency quench valve opens for emergency quench system to reduce the Flue gas temperature.
2. Bypass damper opens &
3. Inlet & Outlet gates are closed.
4. Booster fans are stopped.

D. **SG end Equipment Tripping and its consequence:**

The major equipment tripping at SG end and their consequences are explained below:

1. 1 FD FAN Trip / 1 ID FAN Trip:

When 1 FD Fan Trips, there could be run-back executed at SG end, this will cause the reduction of Boiler Load demand, which will be reflected in IDF's blade pitch control also. Since BUF Blade pitch control follows the IDF Blade Pitch demand, Both BUF will continue to operate with reduced demand.

2. Both FD FAN Trip / Both ID FAN Trip

Both ID/ FD fans trip will lead to unit trip, hence complete FGD system should be shutdown leading to stopping/ tripping of both BUFs and opening of bypass damper.

3. ESP NOT ON/ Not Available:

When the Electrostatic precipitator is not in operation or tripped, this increases dust load in the outlet which will cause serious problem in FGD. Hence FGD GAS-IN should not be permitted, So the By-Pass damper is opened and FGD Automatic Plant shut-down Sequence (APS) is initiated.

CHAPTER NINE

LEARNINGS

1. First six months are very crucial for any project to become successful. In case of a brownfield project, this period can be utilised for clearing fronts for the vendor. If site management of client fails to provide fronts on time, there will always be tussle between client & vendor for the fronts. Vendor will try to prove that all his delays are due to front unavailability. Two FGD plants were awarded by a big client to same vendor at two different brownfield locations. In a case study, where two projects were awarded to same vendor by same client, it was proved that FGD project at one location lagged more than 8 months due to unavailability of fronts.
2. Site Planning & Systems department & Project Execution department shall ensure that in brownfield project, they conduct timely site visits & meetings to survey the area, where new FGD system will be erected. With the help of O&M department, they must clear areas and remove any fouling. Visits by Head of Project helps a lot in clearing fronts.

3. Identification of Site Office area, Storage area, Fabrication yard area & Dumping area by Field Engineering Services before actual mobilisation of Vendor at site helps a lot in avoiding number of future problems.
4. After identification of storage area, only 75% area shall be given to vendor for storage. This will pressurise vendor to avoid non-sequential supply and motivate to stack items properly. In case of emergency, 25% can be given in later stages.
5. In one of the projects, vendor chose structural buildings in place of concrete. But the vendor didn't order the steel structures timely. In pandemic, first the steel prices reduced in initial months after start of pandemic and then skyrocketed in later months. Afterwards there was over 50% increase in the steel prices and vendor was hesitant to order structural items. Vendor failed to take procurement action at the right time. This created cost overrun for the vendor and time overrun for the client. This could be avoided if timely procurement of steel was done by the vendor.
6. Site material management including ensuring sequential supplies, proper stacking, making approaches, proper drains etc. shall be ensured timely. In one of the projects, vendor failed to do these before start of rainy season. Due to heavy rains in area, vendor couldn't retrieve the material due to non-availability of approach for hydra/crane, which resulted in wastage of more than 2 months.
7. Major equipment like Crane arranged by Vendor, while other resource like manpower arranged by Sub-Vendor. In one case study, this mismatch cost

heavily to vendor in Pandemic times. Specially, sub vendor couldn't arrange manpower, but vendor paid rent for heavy machinery. Also sub vendor didn't prioritise augmenting manpower as this monthly rent was not pinching him.

8. Not understanding existing plant priority during construction of brownfield project also creates lots of problem. In one of the projects, while excavation near existing raw water line, the vendor neither provided additional pedestals nor used sheet piling method. Due to this the line started sagging during chimney construction. This delayed the work for more than a month.
9. In one of the plants, 1 meter diameter underground pipeline found during excavation. Due to this fouling, nearly 2 months wasted. FES/ CC-Engg must share underground piping/ cabling etc. details with vendor at the start of project.
10. Vendors must have robust control on sub vendors, and they must have sufficient control measures in contracts awarded to sub-vendors by them. In one of the projects, Vendor gave drawings preparation contract to three parties one after another. The same vendor awarded structure fabrication works to three companies. Structure fabrication companies forced the vendor to revise their Purchase Orders many times. This shows very poor control of sub vendors & internal problem of vendor.
11. So many projects awarded in a very small timeframe, which created demand-supply gap. This resulted in escalation of cost and import of items as sufficient capacity was not available with domestic suppliers. Capacity of A-class construction players exhausted

in initial contracts, which resulted in opting of small companies. This again affected quality and resulted in time overrun. C-276 or other alloy lining, glass lining, Borosilicate lining etc. require specialised manpower and development of such manpower needs time. This delayed nearly all the projects.

12. Tentative quantity of limestone requirement and gypsum generation can be identified in initial phases of project based on selection of technology by vendor. Accordingly, Site shall plan movement of limestone and gypsum within plan premises through Rail/ Road. In case of use of road transportation, planning of movement and strengthening of roads shall be done before actual requirement by FES & Project group.
13. Detail L2 schedule was not available in some projects, which resulted in poor planning & control at site. In one of the projects, Civil work was shown as only one line item in L2. This created problems for Site Planning department as their ability to control things hampered.
14. Many vendors tried first-hand foray into construction without prior experience. Due to equipment supplier mentality and lack of established processes for construction works, construction work delayed in many projects. Small & crucial changes at site were also referred to Head Office by Site manager as very little power was given to him by their corporate office. This created lots of time & cost overrun.
15. Effect of Rain was not considered in L2 schedules, which was not under control of anyone. At one site, due to rains, the work was not possible for more than

15 days in 3 months of rain every year.

16. Murram, filling sand, non-expensive soil etc. are not available during the months of heavy rain. In one of the projects, vendor failed to understand this crucial issue despite numerous guidance from the client and backfilling works were badly affected.
17. Pandemic affected works everywhere. Not retaining workers at site created lots of problem for vendor himself. Poor condition of labour colony added fuel to this fire. Labour mobilisation generally costs nearly five thousand rupees to contractor for each worker. Demobilisation and again mobilisation twice due to two covid waves cost heavily to all vendors. The vendors, who took care of their workers during pandemic were affected less from this effect.
18. Availability of water is also a major issue in construction. Borewells are not allowed as per Environment guidelines. Client shall provide water supply to vendors in place of asking them to arrange themselves.
19. In a running plant, construction sites generally get secondary treatment. Entry of trailers inside plant, unloading of material etc. takes lots of time due to this. This creates lots of problem for vendor as Transporter Companies refuse to transport their material. Security agencies shall be sensitised to avoid this kind of problem and a dedicated person shall be appointed to take care of such issues.
20. In some projects, many a times labour payment was not done timely. This forced labours to stop work or go on strike. This is not only legally but also ethically wrong. All Engineer-In-charges must ensure that labour payment is always done on time. A special

measure like penalty either fixed value or specified % of bill shall be added in contracts to ensure timely payment of labour.

21. Delay in deployment of heavy machinery or deployment of faulty machinery or deployment of incapable machinery also affected the work in some of the plants. Deployment of Tower crane of insufficient capacity delayed works of Electrical Building in one of the projects for nearly 1.5 months.
22. In one of the projects, Ball Mill Erection philosophy was not finalised timely by vendor. Roof casting was delayed for a long time as vendor finalised Ball Mill entry in building by crane from top at a very late stage.

CHAPTER TEN

TYPICAL CALCULATIONS

As the values of parameters are client & vendor specific and proprietary in nature, those can't be used directly in the book without prior permission, which is a tedious process. So, the calculations given assume values and furnish formulas, which can be used by anyone for their specific plant. Some basic change of units, range of vendor furnished parameter etc. explained below.

1. Gas flow at the FGD Inlet = "A" Nm^3/sec
2. Wet Gas flow rate at FGD Inlet = A * 60 * 60 Nm^3/hr
3. Moisture by Volume = "B" %
4. Dry gas flow rate (C) = A * (100 – B)/100
5. BuF Seal Air = "D" Nm^3/hr dry
6. Dry gas flow rate at Absorber Inlet (E) = C + D
7. SO_2Inlet = "F" mg/Nm^3-wet
8. SO_2Inlet (G) = F * 100 / (100 – B) mg/Nm^3-dry
9. SO_2Inlet (H) in ppmd = G / 2.855
10. SO_2concentration (dry basis) (T) = H * E / 1000000 Nm^3/hr
11. Dust = "I" mg/Nm^3

12. Dust loading (dry basis) (J)= I * E / 1000000 kg/hr
13. HCl concentration, as per contract = "K" ppmw
14. HCl concentration (dry basis) (L) = P * 100 /(100-B) ppmd
15. HF concentration, as per contract = "M" ppmw
16. HF concentration (dry basis) (N) = M * 100 /(100-B) ppmd
17. SO_3Concentration (dry basis) = "O" Nm^3/hr
18. SO_2removal efficiency in absorber = "P" %
19. Dust removal efficiency in absorber (W) = "100" %
20. HCl removal efficiency in absorber (X) = "100" %
21. HF removal efficiency in absorber (Y) = "100" %
22. SO_3removal efficiency in absorber = "Q" %
23. Limestone Purity = "R" %
24. Stoichiometry (excess ratio) = "S" %

Excess Ratio is used for SO_3Capture and additional Design considerations and is vendor specific. This is generally in range of 3.5 to 4%.

1. **Limestone Requirement at Design Point:**

a. Absorption of SO_2(U) in Kg/hr = T * (P / 100) * (100/ 22.4)
b. Absorption of HCL (V) in Kg/hr = E * (L / 2) * (X/100) * (100/22.4) * 10^{-6}
c. Absorption of HF (Z) in Kg/hr = E * (N / 2) * (Y/100) * (100/22.4) * 10^{-6}
d. CaCO3 Stoichiometry (a) in Kg/hr = U * S/100
e. Limestone requirement (b) = U + V + Z + a
f. Limestone consumption at Design Point (Kg/hr) (c) = b / (R/100)

2. Gypsum Generation at Design Point:

a. $CaSO_4.2H_2O$ or Gypsum (d) in kg/hr = T * (P/100) * (172/22.4)
b. Unreacted $CaCO_3$ (e) in kg/hr = a
c. Inerts in Limestone (f) in kg/hr = c – b
d. Soluble Alkalies in Limestone (g) in kg/hr = c * (2/100) * (50/100)
e. CaF_2produced by reaction of HF with limestone (h) in kg/hr = E * (N/2) * (Y/100) * (78/22.4) * 10^{-6}
f. Dust in kg/hr = J
g. Gypsum Produced at Design Point (kg/hr) = d + e + f + h + J - g

www.ingramcontent.com/pod-product-compliance
Ingram Content Group UK Ltd.
Pitfield, Milton Keynes, MK11 3LW, UK
UKHW062254290726
14090UKWH00017B/682